Edward Echlin has worked witl
viction to help the church to emt
been to dig deep into the rich soil or tne incarnation. That's what
makes his writing so nourishing, and so prophetic. In this book he
astutely addresses the dangers of climate change to people and
planet alike. Perhaps the greatest risk in this crisis is despair; in
Climate and Christ we have proof of hope.

— Paul Bodenham, Chair, *Christian Ecology Link*

In the light of the unfinished agenda of the Copenhagen
Conference on climate change (2009), this book is timely and
urgent in its message. When scientists, politicians and theologians
agree on an issue of local and global importance, it is time to pay
attention. Edward Echlin's voice in this debate is prophetic, profound and practical.

— Dr Dermot A. Lane, *Mater Dei Institute of Education*, Dublin.

Edward Echlin urges Christians and those wanting to live and act
virtuously at a time of climate change, to 'provide prophetic
alternatives to individualised, consumer, globalised, "growth"
economies which are destroying the earth.' His book provides us
with the confidence to act, knowing that 'prophecy is a viable
alternative to the assumptions and lifestyles of our dominant
cultures."

I strongly recommend this book as a guide for spiritual transformation in tempestuous times.

— Ann Pettifor, Director, *Operation Noah*

Edward P. Echlin

Climate and Christ

A PROPHETIC ALTERNATIVE

the columba press

First edition, 2010, published by
the columba press
55A Spruce Avenue, Stillorgan Industrial Park,
Blackrock, Co Dublin

Cover by Bill Bolger
Origination by The Columba Press
Printed in Ireland by
Colour Books Ltd, Dublin

ISBN 978 1 85607 690-6

Contents

Introduction

> Night shall be thrice night over you,
> And heaven an iron cope.
> Do you have joy without a cause,
> Yea, faith without a hope?
> G. K. Chesterton, *The Ballad of the White Horse*

The threat King Alfred confronted when Danes, 'with horned heads' and 'scarlet beards like blood', swept into Wessex, demanded faith, hope – and resolute damage limitation. The climate crisis, as dramatically demonstrated in the months before, during, and after the disappointing Copenhagen climate summit, with subsequent international tensions, is even more frightening than that which faced Alfred and Wessex.

At the launch of my book *The Cosmic Circle, Jesus and Ecology*, at Sarum College, Dr Mary Grey warned that although I said it would be my last, I had said that before. This book proves Dr Grey right, as is her habit. But why then this book? Because as sea waters, like modern Vikings, rush across shores and into estuaries and, as valiant Maldives islanders and Bangladesh delta people poignantly remind us, our dominant culture of relentless economic growth and global trade, so destabilises the climate as to threaten the very future of life on earth. Jesus and the church – which is Jesus as community today – along with other faiths have much in our tradition to help stem the rising tide and restabilise climate. Surveys now reveal that most people, but by no means all, recognise in their heads, if not in their hearts, that our climate is changing dangerously, that the destabilisation is human-induced through greenhouse gases (ghg), that the whole welcoming biosystem within which we have lived is suffering, and that we must act now and decisively to secure the future of the earth community we have known, including our children. Surveys reveal that although most

people are aware that humans are doing the damage, they still believe the crisis is global, and elsewhere or future, and therefore
they need to change little or not at all. As Al Gore said, when ac-
cepting the Nobel Peace Prize at Oslo, 'The crisis we are facing is
unprecedented – and we often confuse the unprecedented with
the improbable.' Chris Goodall has suggested that humans may
have survived thus far in evolution's struggle because of an innate optimism that insists that all will be well, providing we adapt
for our personal survival ignoring 'the other', including today's
poor and future generations. I am not suggesting, therefore, that
everyone is aware of the extent of our crisis or committed to sustainable living, but that many are, and this is new.

Also new is the revived interest in Charles Darwin. We recently
commemorated anniversaries of Darwin's birth in 1804 and his
celebrated *Origin of Species* in 1859. Despite his own difficulties in
reconciling what he called theism, or faith in God, with his commitment to evolution, Darwin remained open to theism, treasurer
of his local Down, Kent, church, and hoped to be buried, with his
family in Down churchyard. Christians now appreciate Darwin's
discoveries and theories as never before. And we appreciate
Darwin as a warm, vulnerable person, and not merely a detached
observer of species modification, adaptation, natural selection,
survival and extinction. Darwin suffered grievously in his long
life, especially through the untimely death of his daughter Annie.
Even after a century our hearts reach out to him and his wife and
family. Here where I write we also celebrate the centennial of
Pierre Teilhard de Chardin's four years among us, in our local district at Ore Place, Hastings. Chardin, like John Henry Newman,
admired Darwin, becoming convinced of the reality of evolution,
and of 'the evolutive Christ', while here at Hastings. Like Darwin,
Teilhard still profoundly influences our culture.

I offer this book, not for the specialist but for the general and,
like myself, searching readers because the unprecedented (to
adapt Al Gore's word) media coverage of the events, successes,
quarrels, and failures during and since the Copenhagen meetings, have exposed, as never before, the urgency for governments
and individuals (like you and me and our local churches) drastic-

ally to reduce damaging emissions and restabilise climate. It is vitally important for the future of human and all planetary life that governments and industry not only drastically reduce their own emissions, but invest massively in research and development of sustainable alternative energies. In the UK and Ireland, the potential of wind, wave, tidal and, especially in the south and east, of solar energies, are insufficiently appreciated. For both the will, and the many ways, to re-enter creation as sustainably living creatures, the motivation and indeed insistence of religious faith is imperative. More commitment is required than medium term target setting, what Sir Jonathon Porritt calls 'targetitus', with 'cap and trade' and 'carbon trading', and a 'new generation' of so-called clean coal and safe nuclear power stations. We must invest massively in genuine alternative energies, and indeed in alternative ways of living, when old certainties about everlasting growth and 'global trade' are no longer widely accepted. There exists, as climate change becomes evident, continuing interest in world faiths. Within the churches, however, there also persists what we may call a 'forgetfulness of Christ'. Obsessions with 'inner journey' spiritualities flourish, along with debates about church structures, gender, orientations, and leadership. Some easily forget – and certainly do not witness – that we are the Jesus movement. We must remind ourselves that the church, as Christ existing as community today, has a priceless contribution to offer the earth community in its struggle to mitigate climate change and adapt to already irreversible damage. In a word, we have much to offer for the survival of the earth's ecosystems, of society, especially the poor, the church itself, and our children.

In these pages I discuss climate dynamics, which fortunately each of us can influence, at least in small but always important ways. I also discuss evolution including, in this centennial of his years in Britain, Père Teilhard and his vision. I include a chapter on Jesus and his prophetic sustainable lifestyle, which has more to teach and inspire us for prophetic alternative living than previously we, whether Christian or not, may have realised. Finally, and importantly, I conclude with some suggestions for our own prophetic alternative living, including the proximity and in depth principles.

I am grateful to more people than I can mention. Justice dict-ates that I thank, especially, Barbara Echlin, and for making Operation Noah happen – and happen the way it has – Paul Bodenham, Ruth Jarman, Reggie Norton, Ruth and Martin Conway, Ann Pettifor, and Mark Dowd. I also thank Rolf Killingbeck and Marilyn Cummings for invaluable suggestions and help with proof reading; R. J. Berry for kindly providing the reference to Charles Darwin's correspondence with John Fordyce; Drew Dellinger for permission to quote his 'hieroglyphic stairway'; my publisher Seán O Boyle, Columba Press. I respect-fully dedicate these pages to Operation Noah, the leading Christian climate change campaign, which has done – and will do – so much to illuminate heads and touch hearts with the light of Christ that humanity may avoid climate catastrophe.

Edward P Echlin
East Sussex
2010

CHAPTER ONE

Climate Dynamics and Us

The seasons alter: hoary-headed frosts
Fall in the fresh lap of the crimson rose;
And on old Hiems chin and icy crown
An odorous chaplet of sweet summer buds
Is, as in mockery, set: the spring, the summer,
The childing autumn, angry winter, change
Their wonted liveries; and the maz'd world,
By their increase, now knows not which is which:
And this same progeny of evils comes
From our debate, from our dissension:
We are their parents and original.

Shakespeare, *A Midsummer Night's Dream*

With the exception of unrepentant sceptics, most people now recognise that contemporary climate change is driven largely by human actions especially, though not exclusively, by human emissions of greenhouse gases. The technical term for 'human originated' is *anthropogenic*, a mouthful but once you've already grasped *anthropocentric*, as most people now have, you're almost there. *Anthropogenic* means human originated or driven. Our worrying and relentless climate change, we now realise, is caused by anthropogenic emissions, especially from cars, chimneys, planes, ships, buildings, deforestation, and industrial agriculture. Less well integrated into contemporary awareness are the dynamics inherent in climate change. Earth heating, as we know, is mostly caused by our misuse of fossil fuels and by deforestation, intensive agriculture and over-development. But there's more: there are also mutually reinforcing feedbacks resulting from temperature rise, which further accelerate the heating. This means that climate change is not just linear, not as easy to remedy as we once thought, when we 'cut the carbon', imperative though it is for each of us to become at least carbon neutral and live sustainably. For the solar energy the earth receives and what it radiates back into space should be in balance. But since the industrial revolution they are not. We don't radiate back as much radiation as we receive, we retain too much of it. That imbalance is known technically as *radiative forcing*. Previously we thought we could remedy the imbalance between the radiation we receive and what we return by simply reducing the greenhouse gases we emit. Now, however, we're learning it's not that simple – there's another hot chip on the table![1]

Positive and Negative Feedback

That other factor is mutually reinforcing (i.e. amplifying, deleterious) feedbacks. The big worry about these harmful, or positive, feedbacks is that, unlike our emissions, they're not directly and immediately anthropogenic. And they can race beyond our control – they can trigger what's called runaway climate change. If we have the will, we can handle, by reducing our own emissions, what's directly anthropogenic. But the positive feedbacks triggered by our emissions, if we don't counter them immediately can take off on their own as it were, triggered by us and our emissions. That scary 'tipping point' about which scientists talk is a real worry. We may have only a few years to decrease emissions, and equally important, because it's a new challenge, to counter positive feedbacks and to facilitate and even 'be' negative feedback for as long as the harmful positive feedbacks continue. Negative, or damping, mitigating feedback is good; it negates harmful emissions. Negative feedbacks are what we must go for. We must reduce radiative forcing, the imbalance between the radiation earth receives and what it returns to the atmosphere. We do this especially by reducing emissions and through generating our own and other negative feedbacks.

Some principal sources of positive feedbacks which follow our greenhouse gases are: degradation of earth's vital carbon sinks, such as seas, forests, arable soil, and peatfields; discharge of

---

1. David Beerling, *The Emerald Planet, How Plants Changed Earth's History* (Oxford: OUP, 2008), pp 161-162.

powerful methane from warming tundra and sea-beds; decreased *albedo*, a loss of reflection back into space from ice and snow; and an increase of temperature-driven water vapours in the atmosphere. Significantly, an estimated half of our emissions are absorbed by plankton in the now dangerously warming and acidifying oceans, and by soil and plants as a land based sink. Because of warming surface water there are decreased CO_2 emissions absorbed by oceans; and as land sinks are degraded by deforestation, temperature rise, and overdevelopment, those too become sources of emissions, a positive feedback accelerating climate change. Deforestation, especially but not only in the humid tropics, with forest fires and die-back, triggers still more positive feedbacks.

The Arctic and Antarctic are our white canaries, sources of both positive and negative feedbacks as we have noticed. Indeed they are places where we see some efforts to generate helpful negative feedback. In 2008, Sir David King, former government chief scientist and later Director of the Smith School of Free Enterprise and the Environment, told the parliamentary All-Party Climate Change Committee that the summer temperature of 2003, still the hottest on record, will be the norm by 2050, and that we have a lot of adaptation and lifestyle changing to do lest it rise even further thereafter.[2] For us, this means we have a lot of negative feedbacks to facilitate and foster – and to be!

What is befalling Antarctica, the Arctic and Alaska is a dramatic white warning of what lies ahead unless people immediately and drastically reduce their addiction to fossil fuel burning. Journalist Mark Lynas visited Alaska in 2003 and, unlike then Governor Sarah Palin, noticed that,

Alaska is baking. Temperatures in the state – as in much of the Arctic – are rising ten times faster than in the rest of the world. And the effects are so dramatic that entire ecosystems are beginning to unravel, as are the lifestyles of the people –many of them Native Americans – who depend on them. In many ways

2. Sue Meredith Velado, 'AAPPCCG Meeting Jointly with APUD', *Living Green* (September 2008), p 47.

Alaska is the canary in the coal mine, showing the rest of the world what lies ahead as global warming accelerates.[3]

Few historical or even planetary events – at least so far! – are completely unprecedented. Our planet has experienced climate change and extinctions before. Independent scientist James Lovelock notes climate change in geological history:

Change is a normal part of geological history; the most recent was the earth's move from the long period of glaciation to the present warmish interglacial. What is unusual about the coming crisis is that *we* are the cause of it, and nothing so severe has happened since the long hot period at the start of the Ecocene, fifty-five million years ago, when the change was larger than that between the ice age and the nineteenth century and lasted for 200,000 years.[4]

Iron Age people were unaware of climate dynamics as such, but Hebrew leaders knew that human misbehaviour could result in capricious weather. The prophet Jeremiah (c. 600BC) for example warned:

This people has a stubborn and rebellious heart; they have turned aside and gone away. They do not say in their hearts, 'Let us fear the lord our God, who gives the rain in its season, the autumn rain and the spring rain, and keeps for us the weeks appointed for the harvest.' Your iniquities have turned these away, and your sins have kept good from you (Jer 5:23-25; cf Deut 11:13f).

In recovering the ecological riches in the Bible, and in subsequent tradition, we must be aware of our different, ever changing contexts. The climate context during which Jeremiah, and the priestly tradition and, later, Jesus and Paul lived was different from our own. Our climate dynamics are adversely influenced by human malfeasance. We depend on climate scientists, who are respected by peers and environmentalists and who, as far as

3. Mark Lynas, *High Tide, How Climate Crisis is Engulfing Our Planet* (NY: Harper Perennial, 2004), p 39.
4. James Lovelock, *The Revenge of Gaia* (London: Allen Lane, 2006), p 7.

human power can discern, are reliable. Science, however, keeps changing as new evidence is discovered and as contexts change. Ian Barbour, respected writer on science and religion, notes that science itself is historically conditioned. Indeed we know more about climate dynamics now than we did in 1992 and 2009. Even when we consult reliable scientists about what science and what evidence is compelling, that will soon change. The science accepted at the Copenhagen Summit in 2009 will soon change, as did that accepted at Rio in 1992. Successive IPPC reports, for example, always include new evidence, and by the time governments learn, discuss, and act upon that evidence – if indeed they do act – the evidence may be ten years out of date. Nevertheless, there are significant, substantial, and worrying 'facts on the ground' and in the atmosphere which we may usefully discuss here.

Along with the science of earth heating, we also have our own and other peoples' experience of strange weather and food growing difficulties. Sir Ghillean Prance noted, when we lectured together to a Christian NGO at Crawley, that everywhere he went as Director of Kew Gardens people reported strange weather. Similarly, Mark Lynas recalls telling a young Alaskan what he was researching as a working journalist. The young man observed that winter was coming later and spring sooner. Instead of migrating south, ducks swam on rivers all winter. Bears hibernated fitfully or not at all. And people were worried because at Christmas one year it rained and melted the snow.[5]

That suffering, of animals and people, is painful for all committed to a Creator who cares for ourselves and our fellow earth creatures of sea and land. This chapter, in other words, is more than a description of climate change which is now obvious to most people. We who are concerned with climate dynamics and with the effects on creation of climate change, cannot overlook the suffering of our fellow creatures inherent in climate change; and with attention to that suffering, our responsibility to discover, facilitate, and even to be negative feedback.

---

5. Lynas, *High Tide*, p 38.

The Wisdom of Food Growing

It is instructive 'popular science' to wander around allotments, where soil students are welcome, to discover the precious wisdom of many allotment holders and, indeed, to learn from the wisdom inherent in the whole soil community of plants and animals (Is 28:23-29; Job 12:9). Even before I realised the gravity of climate dynamics and the effect of climate change on food production and security, I visited allotments and asked experienced holders about their choice of crops and how their vegetables, fruit, and sometimes fowl, protected themselves from unwelcome parasites and predators. For allotments are usually beyond sight of a holder's home. Wood pigeons, for example, are now a major brigand as a new generation of home owners, some also owners of one or more large vehicles with scant sensitivity towards the earth and earth's limits, now cover even front gardens with pavement and shingle. Entrepreneurs with mini-vans engage in 'ground construction', a euphemism for scraping up gardens, once appreciated and tended, and replacing grass and plants with pavements, slabs, plastic, and gravel. Large rear gardens too, some with trees and former vegetable plots, are now classified as 'grey land' by earth illiterate politicians and civil servants, enabling gardens, like tiled front garden car parks, to be concreted, 'decked', and even built upon. These destructive, cruel, unsustainable activities deprive urban wildlife of habitats, hence the attraction of allotments to wood pigeons, jays, badgers, rabbits, and other fruit and vegetable consumers. Allotment holders must also protect their crops from cabbage butterflies and caterpillars, slugs and snails, and hungry birds. When I enquire about the weather, veteran holders, as Sir Ghillean Prance noted about his travels, report unusual weather – and climatic – irregularities since they began food growing. To cite an example here in the south east, they report that they use more water during increasing dry spells than they once did. Some growers, lacking a mains outlet, now carry water as well as tools to their plots. Further west, reports differ; veteran holders report too much summer rain, and sometimes plant crushing winter floods.

My own garden serves as another amateur ecologist's school and, effectively, an eco-theologian's workplace and instructor, inviting Ignatian contemplation of Jesus in the main part of his life, at Nazareth where he too worked with the soil in family fields. Because I am not an allotment holder, people ask the size of my patch. On open garden days, increasing numbers of newly interested food growers view and study it, as I do the allotments. Including house, garage, shed, and small yard, I garden about a third of an acre, equivalent to two large allotments, plus hedges, fences and walls. I grow about ninety fruit varieties, including suitable varieties on north and east facing walls and fences. We grow not just seasonal summer and autumn crops, which eaten fresh are a luxury for growers no matter how small their patch, we also grow fruit and vegetables for the long winter, such as potatoes, kale and top fruit keepers. Barbara quickly fills the small freezer with runner and broad beans; and then preserves in kilners pears, plums, gooseberries, currants, and mixed fruit; and also produces chutneys, pickles, and jellies. As John Seymour insisted, 'complete' self sufficiency is a fiction, but partial self sufficiency is an important way to heal the suffering of the earth inherent in climate change. Partial self-sufficiency is an important way to involve ourselves in climate dynamics, because smallscale food production can contribute to climate stabilisation. Fortunately food growing and fascination with self sufficiency is now returning, especially since the 'credit crunch' and the awareness raising and dire warnings at the Copenhagen summit about the globalised 'world trade' spree, until recently encouraged even by aid organisations and 'fair traders'. Here, we are reasonably, if only partly, self sufficient in fruit and vegetables, supplementing these from farmers' markets of which we have two monthly, and other local and free-range outlets. Time and space do not permit domestic animals, except for our peke Mildred, an indispensable companionable visual aid, who represents, with panache, during lectures our sensate covenant partners (Gen 9:8-17).

In the four decades I have gardened in the UK, I have noticed numerous climate related changes. Not all weather changes are pernicious, however, at least in the short term. In 2008 and 2009, for example, we harvested peppers and currant tomatoes well into November, almost until American Thanksgiving (the fourth Thursday in November). When long nights and the occasional light frost finally closed in I uprooted plants laden with immature green peppers which Barbara froze for winter casseroles. Even in winter our solar panels accommodate fridge and freezer needs during daylight, and at night we draw from our deposit in the grid. Late peppers and tomatoes are not the only climate related novelty I've noticed. I used to plant fruit during the first week of November. Then nurserymen began lifting plants later, as dormancy began later. Now I'm planting in January. Formerly I planted first early potatoes on St Patrick's Day, and seconds on Maundy Thursday. Then I began to plant both on 12 March, a traditional feast of the Jesuit missionary Francis Xavier, and to lift them gradually, as needed, from early June. I lift the remnant in late July because blight traditionally sweeps through despite the coastal winds. In brief, except for those blight-driven July liftings, I grow and eat potatoes weeks earlier than we did last century.

Another disturbing symptom is new growth and occasional autumn blossom on fruit trees. The crisp autumn nights and ground frosts are missing. I also notice on allotments, when holders have not repeatedly rubbed out caterpillars, that brassicas are virtually demolished. There are also fewer tits in gardens, despite attempts to accommodate them with birdhouses and protected feeders. Tits assist gardeners by eating aphid eggs on branches in winter. George Marshall notices, 'Wildlife will change dramatically. Those animals whose lifecycles are dependent on regular seasons will be severely affected. To cite just one example, blue tit populations are falling because their nesting season is no longer synchronised with the appearance of the caterpillar larvae they need to feed their young.'[6] Another loss, less attributable to climate change than to a principal cause of climate change, is the decline of companionable slug devouring hedgehogs, victims of hit and run boy racers. I occasionally see dead hedgehogs on road edges in the morning, killed instantly by drivers who didn't even stop. I have buried two hit-and-run hedgehog victims in my garden, where even in death they continue to serve the soil community. Also in decline are the thrushes and amphibians which, with

6. George Marshall, *Carbon Detox, Your Step-by-Step Guide to Getting Real About Climate Change* (London: Aclypus Publishing, 2007), p 73.

hedgehogs, reduce slug and snail predation.

I should also mention some other recent especially extreme weather conditions for gardeners. Heavy summer rain and floods in 2007/2008, for example, made gardening difficult especially in flood prone regions. In July 2007, I noticed swans swimming blissfully on flooded Christ Church meadow, Oxford, where cattle still roam, and where John Macquarrie, when Lady Margaret Professor, walked with his young family on summer evenings. While we cannot relate all strange weather to human interference with climate, extreme droughts – as in April and May 2008 and 2009 – and summer floods are warning signals that can make us pause. As long ago as 1994, Sir John Houghton, former chair of the IPCC working group, acknowledged the uncertain causes of some floods and droughts, hedging his comments with 'may', 'probably', and 'likely', but Houghton left no doubt that the 'business as usual' approach of many politicians and industrialists is dangerous. The 'back to growth' attitude of most world leaders during the 2009-2010 recession, and the sombre predictions of scientists since Copenhagen of where we are heading, and of what even a 4° temperature rise will bring, confirm Houghton's warnings. The 'precautionary principle' is the sensible way to proceed. That is, when human actions, especially our own, 'may' or 'likely' affect climate adversely, even if we are not certain they do, we should take precautions and ascertain that we are living within earth's restraints. In John Houghton's words,

> Many ecosystems (including human beings) may not be able to adapt easily to such a rate of change. The most noticeable impacts are likely to be on the availability of water (especially on the frequency and severity of droughts and floods) and on the distribution (though possibly not on the overall size) of global food production. Further, although most of our predictions have been limited in range to the end of next century, it is clear than by the century beyond 2100 the magnitude of the change in climate and the impacts resulting from that change are likely to be very large indeed.[7]

7. John Houghton, *Global Warming, The Complete Briefing* (Oxford: Lion Publishers, 2004), p 129.

Even before the industrial revolution, when fossil fuel extraction and burning proliferated, there were, as geology, archaeology, the Bible, and other ancient written records testify, intermittent floods and droughts, as well as protracted glacial and interglacial periods. Human behaviour may have contributed to the intensity of floods and droughts, while not being the major cause. There was, for example, the release of carbon and methane induced by widespread neolithic deforestation. But in general there existed a dynamic balance between solar radiation received and that which the earth radiated back into the atmosphere. What makes for a climatic 'earth in balance' is plentiful negative feedback countering or balancing radiation received and positive feedbacks. The respected James Hansen of the Goddard Space Studies Institute says, 'The earth's climate is remarkably sensitive to global forcings. Positive (amplifying) feedbacks predominate. This allows the entire planet to be whipsawed between climate states. Recent greenhouse gas emissions place the earth perilously close to dramatic climate change that could run out of our control.'[8]

Hansen implies a difference between anthropogenic emission and the resultant positive feedbacks that together are heating our planet. The latter, such as warming seas absorbing less CO_2, follow human induced global heating but are not directly induced. Positive feedback is a daunting challenge. Every degree of climate change results in an estimated ten per cent decline in global food production. In the meetings preceding Copenhagen, and at the summit itself and since, sober estimates of projected heating if countries do not reduce emissions by at least 40% by 2020, range from 2° to a frightful 6°.[9] We must not only live sustainably locally ourselves, we must discover and implement and support negative feedbacks which counter anthropogenic damage and positive feedbacks. I submit that negative feedback is a mission of

8. In Peter Cox, Deepak Rughani, PeterWadhams, David Wasdell, *Planet Earth, We Have a Problem, Feedback Dynamics and the Acceleration of Climate Change* (Leeds: Angus Print, 2007), p 10.
9. Stockholm Environment Institute and Friends of the Earth, *Europe's Share of the Climate Challenge: Domestic Actions and International Obligations to Protect the Planet* (30 November 2009, www.sei-international.org).

Christian churches and all faiths in our time. This challenge, unique to our generation, will preoccupy us in different ways for the remainder of this book.

Water Disarray

As I write on the UK south coast, sea defences are being built, while in this southeast corner summer drought interferes with food production, aquifers, and resources. Drought with concomitant hunger ravages East Africa, including northern Kenya, Ethiopia, Uganda, and Somalia. The UN estimates 17 million people are on the verge of famine. Small farmers in north east Ethiopia urge a return to traditional small scale and sustainable growing. In Catalonia, Spain, grass watering and car washing with potable water, environmentalist say belatedly, is forbidden. Proposed fixes for water shortages include carbon emitting desalination and piped water from the Rhone and Ebro. These fail to address the root causes of climate change, including fossil fuel burning and aquifer disruption, to which the Spanish themselves and their transient villa owners, expatriates and tourists contribute. There is talk of 'water wars' but not of climate and water peace. Also in the Mediterranean region, poignantly, the Jordan is so over-extracted, polluted, and diminished, especially by illegal west bank settlements, that an Israel based NGO, 'Zalul', campaigns to restore and protect the sacred river. The Israeli water authority warns that the very future of the Sea of Galilee as a fresh water lake is threatened. Unsuspected by previous generations there are saline springs on the lake's floor dangerously diluting the diminished fresh water. Further north, in the UK I have gardened through three withering droughts, accompanied by hosepipe bans, exacerbated by the dry micro-climate of this strip of the southeast coast, which dry climate, according to the UK Met Office, is predicted to continue as climate change worsens. Burning drought in the southeast is good for photovoltaic electricity generation but bad for food growing and human health. Africa, southern Spain, Galilee, and occupied Palestine, and even this strip of coast near Hastings, may be harbingers of what fossil fuel addiction does to the earth. Theologian Michael Northcott observes:

There is growing evidence that the increased frequency and severity of drought in sub-Saharan and South Africa in the last ten years is a consequence not just of local climate change but of anthropogenic global warming. Scientists report a general drying of the African continent from the Mediterranean coast to the Cape of Good Hope, and they note the spread of sand dunes from the Sahara and Kalahari deserts across Northern and Central Africa. Desertification south of the Sahara in the Sahel may also be a consequence of rising temperatures in the Indian Ocean and not just of overgrazing. Extensive famine in the region in the last twenty years is quite possibly the first major human catastrophe consequent on human-induced climate change.[10]

Droughts, whether in my garden, southern Europe, East and North Africa, or southeast Australia are all related – in climate 'all things are connected' – to the ominous melting of sea ice, glaciers and tundra throughout the earth. There are, or will soon be, according to UN estimates, over 200 million environmental refugees. Arctic ice shrinkage is measured by satellites, the core thinning is monitored by submarines. Loss of snow and ice in the Arctic, Antarctic, Greenland, and the mountain glaciers is a positive feedback affecting *albedo*. Warming oceans and land lead literally to food insecurity and other positive feedbacks. Peter Wadhams, an ocean climate dynamics specialist, explains:

The summer reduction of sea ice is now clearly visible from satellites. It is probably the clearest aspect of global warming that is visible from space. We can see that there are huge expanses now of the Beaufort Sea and the areas north of Russia which are ice-free in summer, which have never been before. So this not only results in increased evaporation, but also in a very much decreased average global *albedo*. When you have an ice or snow cover it reflects about 80%-90% of incident solar short-wave radiation straight back into space. But as soon as you take that ice cover away and replace it with ocean, the re-

---

10. Michael Northcott, *A Moral Climate, the Ethics of Global Warming* (London: DLT, 2007), p 31.

flection goes down to about 10%. So we are absorbing a lot more radiation at the earth's surface and this is accelerating the rate of global warming.[11]

The crowded urbanising world, no less than Greenland, depends on winter freezes to replenish summer thaws. When thaws exceed winter's replacement freezing, the open ocean reflects less radiation than does ice and snow, another positive feedback. Around Greenland's coasts the thaw of contiguous ocean ice accelerates tundra thawing which in turn emits methane. Significantly, small boats formerly icebound until late June now embark in May.

While in Alaska, Mark Lynas noted the rural wisdom and experience of indigenous people who realise that, despite denial of oil companies and politicians, Alaska climate is already changing, even faster than in southern states. Sexagenarian grandfather, Clifford Weyiouanna, knows the Seward Peninsula well, a bare hundred miles from Siberia, the ancient migration trail of west bound primitive people, a long way from air conditioned Las Vegas. Clifford told Lynas that the currents and the thickness of ice on the Chukchi Sea had changed. The turquoise blue icebergs from the north no longer approached. Ice that in the past would have been four feet thick was now only about a foot thick. The large mammals, including the polar bears, the walrus, the spotted seal, the bearded seal, the belugas and the bowhead whales were all migrating north in spring to stay in the cooler waters.[12]

Melting mountain glaciers in Asia similarly deprive people dependent on some major world rivers of drinking, irrigation and sanitation water, including the millions dependent on the Ganges and Yangtse. Nicholas Grey, founder of Wells for India, and knowledgeable in Eurasian hydrology, predicts famine for millions if earth heating melts Himalayan glaciers. The IPCC and the UN warn that by 2050 millions may be displaced by flooding.[13] Already Bangladesh aquifers and fields are becoming salinated.

11. In Cox et al, Planet Earth, We Have a Problem, p 77.
12. Lynas, High Tide, pp 50-51.
13. IPCC, 'Climate Change Impacts, Technical Summary', (Geneva: 2007).

Inward migrations to India have begun. Similar catastrophes will affect the Nile and other deltas. [14] In Britain, even if changes in the Gulf Stream deflect earth heating, a cooler Britain could attract massive unsustainable migrations. Already, with melting northern sea ice and ocean warming, here on the Channel (*La Manche*) where I garden, migrating sea species including red mullet, cuttle fish and squid are colonising, and sea bass are increasing. Peter Wadhams observes:

> The thing of which we are certain is that the sea surface temperature is rising globally, and this is decreasing the density of sea water and causing the ocean to stand higher. One example of ocean warming has been locally here in the North Sea. The North Sea winter temperatures have gone up by more than a degree in the last few decades and this is one of the reasons why the cod is disappearing from the North Sea because it is becoming too warm for cod to spawn. [15]

Flooding, with ocean warming and acidification extinguishes species on sea and land. Acidification reduces surface algae and plankton which formerly absorbed CO_2 emissions. In developed countries such as densely populated Britain, which has already destroyed much of its fertile soil for 'development' including roads, housing, airports, industrial agriculture, and 'brownfield' gardens, sea level rise will diminish arable land further. This, coupled with similar soil destruction in developing countries, adds urgency to re-enter creation by living sustainably and symbiotically with climate as individuals and communities, especially in urban areas which produce most emissions. Mayor Richard Daley of Chicago, in fertile northern Illinois, warned that without immediate and drastic changes, Chicago itself, which would have been unthinkable when I studied there, could become as arid as Texas.

Forests
An important contribution to earth heating and desertification is

---

14. Houghton, *Global Warming*, pp 94-95.
15. In Cox *et al*, *Planet Earth We Have A Problem*, p 88.

continuing deforestation with its concomitant reduction of bio-diversity. The eminent biologist E. O. Wilson estimates that 50,000 years ago the rate of animal species extinction was about one per million annually. Now he estimates the rate is possibly one thous-and per million annually. Extinction is related to woodland clear-ance. In the UK, already one of the least wooded countries in the EU, a dalesman farmer pointed out to me a densely wooded fell on his farm. 'It used to be all like that', he commented, 'before the dales were deforested and intensively grazed.' Along with many sensitive farmers, landowners and NGOs, the Woodland Trust preserves some remaining ancient woodlands, and replants and restores others. Here near Burwash, where Rudyard Kipling's son who fell in the Great War is commemorated in market square, we dedicated, through the Woodland Trust, a small glade of ancient chestnut, perhaps planted in Norman times, to Barbara's late father Jack Larkin, himself a planter of trees. Recently the Trust pur-chased the 649 acre Brede High Wood in Sussex, now their largest site in England, a mixture of ancient woods and heathland, home to some rare species including wild boar, great crested newts, and a rare leaf beetle. The Trust also preserves 870 acre West Wood, their largest in Wales, a habitat to lizards, deer, and woodland birds. In Kent, near where the Romans landed, the Trust restored Victory Wood, previously destined for landfill. According to the Trust, 506 ancient woods are still endangered, significantly 173 are threatened by yet more ruinous road building, and 69 by un-sustainable green field housing.[16] The 1.3 million pounds budgeted for widening the M25, attracting more traffic and emissions, would plant 3.2 million carbon absorbing street trees.

People in northern Europe and America can assist those in the humid tropics struggling to preserve forests, such as Renato de Jesus in Brazil and Kevin Conrad in Papua, New Guinea.[17] For the southern forests are (literally) vitally important for the symbiosis

16. Peter Marren, *Britain's Ancient Woodland Heritage* (London: David & Charles, 1990), p 10.

17. Joseph E. Stiglitz, 'Kevin Conrad. He took on the US government and proved that smaller nations can lead the way in fighting climate change', *Time* (6 October 2008), pp 58-59.

and health of the entire earth community, including our own children. Tropical deforestation and its aftermath account for an estimated 20% of global CO_2 emissions. An area about the size of Flanders is felled annually. Deforestation of old growth rain-forests, as in Brazil, including scattered 'breaks' or gaps in forests caused by mining, oil exploration, and small scale ranching, trigger 'ecosystem failure' such as we see on a smaller scale in over-development in the developed world. Biodiverse communities cease to contribute their services, including carbon sequestration. In South America there is diminished transpiration of rain and mists which contribute to rain for western South America and the western states. A major cause of wanton deforestation is industrial logging and subsequent monocultures of soya and palm oil,

> Rapidly growing economies such as China are scouring the world for timber and other forest products. China now buys 55 per cent of the Republic of Congo's timber exports, which come almost entirely from virgin forests. Increasingly, not only timber but also palm oil and soybeans are being imported from ecologically vulnerable rainforest regions. Malaysia is supplying ever-growing amounts of palm oil from converted rainforests. In 2006 it exported some 14.4 million tonnes of palm oil, and of this China imported nearly 3.6 million tonnes. In the last 20 years China has become the world's largest im-porter of whole soybeans as well as oil and meal by-products. Brazilian soy exports to China, mainly from the Amazon and former savannah regions in Mato Grosso, increased from one million tons to four million tons between 1999 and 2003.[18]

The fires endemic in deforestation further diminish absorp-tion and transmission of moisture, and tragically become them-selves another contributor to earth heating. Smoke from fires in the Brazilian Amazon, for example, inhibit the penetration of light and gentle heat which normally drive the transpiration pro-cess which makes Argentina fertile, and penetrates even further north. Tropical forests store many gigatons of carbon. Amazonia alone stores 120. We should also notice Asian peatlands, like Amazonia being stripped and monocropped for 'biofuel' for omnivorous American cars. As a result of the exploitation in Amazonia and Asia, even if Europe reduced its own emissions, as we must, by 80% to 90%, but cannot reverse deforestation, the earth community's future is bleak. We must also help and encourage indigenous people to use their wisdom and experience to conserve, manage and, where necessary, restore tropical forests. We must halt our own deforestation and road building, and assist individuals and groups, such as the Woodland Trust, to reforest and replant our own woodland. In 2007 and 2009 the Woodland Trust planted two million trees, providing an incentive and example to other organisations and to industrialists. As Richard Smithers of the Woodland Trust says, 'What we need to do is manage whole landscapes sympathetically for wildlife and for people.' Biodiversity, especially when symbiotic with food production, is also symbiotic with climate.

Food Landscapes
As we noticed, even stone age farmers sometimes damaged their environment, although with sustainable populations and primitive technologies – the hoe being their best herbicide – they did not damage climate as do their successors.[19] Food growers, large and small, are living barometers of weather vagaries and climate who, unlike wall barometers, in ways large and small can and do influence it. Hence the carbon sequestration of our organic farms and gardens. To use an intimate example from my own relatively small organic garden, I have long grown – and save seeds of – a scrambling currant tomato and a traditional cos lettuce. Almost unbelievably, compared to a few decades ago, I now harvest currant tomatoes into November, albeit from blackening vines. The shiny cos, formerly grown for the March hunger gap, were often nipped by winter frosts. No longer, as the winters milden. Instead these now mature and bolt in autumn well before they're needed. What Shakespeare called 'old Hiems' icy brow' no longer frowns

19. Christopher Southgate, *The Groaning of Creation, God, Evolution, and the Problem of Evil* (London: Westminster John Knox Press, 2008), p 98.

with cold as it formerly did. The climate destabilisation noticed by urban and exurban growers, the myriad small scale gardeners and allotment growers, is shared by farmers. Sandra Nichols, of the National Farmers' Union, observes that 60% of farmers report that climate change impacts their fields.[20] Blackcurrant growers find that winters are no longer hard enough for some traditional varieties and experiment, as do other fruit growers, with 'climate change crops'. The IPCC predicts ominously that yields could fall by 50% as soon as 2020, a year targeted for reductions of green-house gas emissions at the UN Mexico summit. Some models pre-dict 30% reduction in cereals and 18% in maize across Africa. The UN Food and Agriculture Forestry and Fisheries Organization (FAO) says reduced rainfall impacts farmers everywhere and 'croplands, pastures and those least able to cope will likely bear additional adverse impacts'. Miguel Altieri, a respected authority on sustainable agriculture, warns:

> The pressures are setting in motion a global food system crisis of unprecedented scope that is already signalled by food riots in many parts of the world. It threatens the livelihoods of mil-lions more than the current 850 million hungry people, and is the direct result of the dominant industrial farming model – a model dangerously dependent on fossil fuels and the largest source for human impact on the biosphere.[21]

Nearly 90% of the world's 1.5 billion acres of arable land – excluding organic farms, holdings, allotments, and gardens – em-ploy oil-derived inputs and irrigation water. Subsidised mono-cultures, with their inherent vulnerability to climate change and their lack of soil replenishment, threaten world food supplies. Alarmed by climate change, richer countries and corporations, including India, China, and Gulf emirates, are buying millions of acres of cropland in some of the world's poorest countries. Food prices everywhere, even in richer economies, increasingly chal-lenge family budgets. Altieri comments:

20. Lorna Train, 'Climate Change Conference', *Sussex Review*, CPRE (Summer 2008), p 7.
21. Miguel Altieri, 'Small Farms Show Big Progress', *Food Ethics* (Autumn 2008), pp 22-24.

Climate change has reduced crop yields as a result of droughts, floods, and other unpredictable weather events. Expanding land areas devoted to biofuels and transgenic crops are further exacerbating the ecological footprint of vast monocultures. Moreover, industrial agriculture contributes at least one-quarter of current greenhouse gas emissions, mainly methane and nitrous oxide. Continuing this dominant degrading system, as promoted by the current economic paradigm, is no longer a viable option.[22]

Yet, despite the vast chemical monoculture of industrial farming, including that devoted to transgenic crops and biofuels for cars, millions of small growers still feed millions of people. Small growers, both rural and in settlements, are labour intensive and climate symbiotic. Small growers undoubtedly provide the example and 'way of proceeding' we need in our climate and food crunch. In Latin America, for example, about 17 million small growers, on farms of less than two hectares, produce 5% of the maize, 99% of the legumes, and 61% of the potatoes grown there. In hungry Africa, about 30 million small producers, with farms of less than two hectares, produce food for local consumption, contrasting with large farms, being bought up by neo-colonial 'land grabbers', who export their produce, including precious 'virtual water'. In Asia, 20 million small farms of less than two hectares produce most Asian rice. We owe an inestimable debt to small growers everywhere who produce grain, vegetables, fruit, fodder, fowl, dairy, and meat products, and whose yield per unit, exceeds that of intensive agriculture.

Small farmers and growers have a personal interest in their local biosystem, reducing soil erosion and conserving biodiversity, thereby helping stabilise climate. As world populations and food tensions continue to increase, the care and resilience of small growers may be the best, if not only way to feed a warming world with dwindling arable soil, water, and symbiotic climate. As HRH Prince Charles said in the 2008 Sir Albert Howard Memorial Lecture:

---

22. Ibid.

I want to see trust being put back in individual farmers, with their knowledge of the land and their skills honed over generations, and thus helping them find the sustainable solutions which respect – rather than upset – nature's natural balance. After all, just as the myriad of small businesses are the mainstay of any economy, so are small family farmers the backbone, the lifeblood and the guardians of the rural environment.

Small farmers and growers, with urban growers, provide carbon sinks and are a source of negative feedback. Organic soils, with accompanying hedges, trees, and vegetables, absorb and sequester carbon and do not emit nitrous oxides. Research suggests that conversion of more medium and small farms and gardens to organic production would sequester carbon equivalent to removing 1,174,000 cars from the road.[23]

A remarkable multi-government 'International Assessment of Agriculture, Science and Technology for Development' (IAASTD) after four years of study involving many governments, the World Bank, and 40 scientists, concluded that conventional farming has concentrated on quantity of production and neglected earth's restraints. The report describes the relationship between climate change and agriculture as 'a two-way street, agriculture contributes to climate change in several major ways, and climate change in general adversely affects agriculture.' IAASTD specifies the impact on food of floods and droughts, and of migrating pests and diseases; and the resultant conflicts over land and water. We already see conflict over migrations and rich nations, large and small, 'colonising' by buying agricultural land in Asia and Africa. 'There is serious potential for future conflicts over habitable land and natural resources such as fresh water. Climate change is affecting the distribution of plants, invasive species, pests, and disease vectors and the geophysical range and incidence of many human, animal, and plant diseases is likely to increase.' Significantly, and widely noticed, was IAASTD's recognition of the importance of small farms and holdings, organic cultivation, agroforestry and reforestation, with the reduction of

23. Ibid, p 23.

artificial fertilisers and biofuel production. Small scale farming – with urban food cultivation – which absorbs rather than contributes to CO_2 could be a major contributor to restabilisation of climate. In brief, IAASTD, while not rejecting large farms, recognises that small, sustainable, biodiverse, carbon sequestering farms and holdings are the optimum way to feed a growing population while also mitigating climate change,

> Sustainable agriculture products are part of the solution to current environmental change. Examples include improved carbon storage in soil and biomass, reduced emissions of CH_4 and N_2O from rice paddies and livestock, and decreased use of inorganic fertilisers. Appropriate policies can promote mitigation of greenhouse gas emissions and increased carbon sequestration.[24]

Farmers are experimenting with drought resistant cereals. Some varieties are preserved in the world's seed banks, including Heritage Seed Savers (Warwickshire, UK), Irish Seed Savers Association (Scariff, Co Clare), and Seed Savers Exchange (Iowa). Unfortunately, precious seed banks in Iraq and Afghanistan were destroyed in what Bruce Kent prophetically calls the endemic unpredictability of war. Another seed bank, in the Philippines, was damaged by an earthquake. When seed saver and 'grower out' Jean de Berthelot began 'growing out' rare seedlings in tiny beds in Lot Garonne, he could find only 17 cultivated wheat varieties even in garden France. After searching the world's seed banks, he now 'grows out' 200 varieties, some of them drought resistant, others providing ground cover or 'mulch' as well as grain. These seeds are now stored in the seed bank at Spitzberg, Norway. Of peasant growers everywhere, Sir Julian Rose notes, 'Peasant farmers are the last line of absolute resistance to the global corporate take over of the food chain. The red blood that runs through their veins is the most valuable human asset mankind possesses – it is quite literally the key to our survival as sentient, loving, human beings.'[25] The local indigenous wisdom of small growers,

24. http://wwww.greenfacts.org/em//1-2//.small-farmers-trade.htm
25. Sir Julian Rose, 'GM Crops and Eugenics', *Fourth World Review* (October 2008), pp 7-8.

handed on for centuries, includes extended family cohesion and
sharing within communities, as the Jewish scriptures teach. The
Millennium Ecosystem Assessment noted that climate change
threatens to erase this priceless local wisdom.[26]

Peasant farmers and growers and 'growers out' like Jean de
Berthelot, and participating members of seed savers' associations,
struggle to maintain local diversity within the unprecedented restraints of anthropogenic climate change. Water harvesting skill
is also necessary. Dr Nicholas Grey observes, 'It is becoming increasingly clear that smallscale water-harvesting will be a key
tool to help the rural poor adjust to climate changes not only in
India but also across other parts of Asia, across Africa and South
America'.[27] Recently the government of New South Wales was
compelled to restrict irrigation of the Murray Darling Basin. The
Darling river and underground aquifers diminish, and the Great
Barrier Reef is bleaching. Yet air conditioning and air miles addicted Australia contributes a disproportionate 7% of global greenhouse gases, and is the earth's fifth highest *per capita* emitter. This
denial and climate abuse can – and must – change, especially considering Australian and American genuine wealth of Pacific sun,
and potential wind, ocean, air and geo-thermal energies.
Australian Tim Flannery writes, 'We are the generation fated to
live in the most interesting of times, for we are now the weather
makers, and the future of biodiversitiy and civilisation hangs on
our actions.'[28]

Conclusion

Agriculture, large and very small, with water harvesting, is a
splendid high point on which to conclude. For millions of people,
in settlements and in rural areas, are again listening to William
Cecil's advice to 'have a little land around you', even if that little

26. Jonathan Ensor and Rachel Berger, *Understanding Climate Change,
Adaptation Lessons from Community Based Approaches* (Rugby: Practical
Action Publishing, 2009), pp 2-3.
27. Nicholas Grey, 'Climate Change in India', *Wells for India Newsletter* (No
46, Summer 2009), p 6.
28. Tim Flannery, *The Weather Makers, The History and Future Impact of
Climate Change* (London: Penguin, 2005), p 306.

land is just that – a few metres of front garden, or less. Unsurprisingly, after decades of building on green fields and declaring gardens 'brown' fields open to developers, there are now long waiting lists for scandalously scarce allotments. People increasingly, whether in care homes, schools, small holdings, farms, or exurbia, are sowing that 'little land' for which each is especially responsible. More are growing a little food, and sequestrating a little carbon, making our small but cumulatively significant contribution to stabilisation of weather and climate.[29] We facilitate negative feedbacks which counter anthropogenic climate change and subsequent positive feedbacks. About 10,000 years ago when our species learned to collect, sow, and save seeds, and to cultivate 'a little land', we launched the anthropocene era wherein we, women and men together, became and are, in Flannery's phrase 'the weather makers'. All nations must collaborate as the world community we are. Climate, no less than our shared humanity and frail creaturehood has made us a community. Anthropogenic climate change, which is caused by all, both so-called developed and developing people, causes deplorable suffering and even extinction of earth's creatures. So does, in its different way, the whole evolutionary process to which we now turn.

---

29. John Neal, 'A Farmers' Reflections', *Countryside Care, The Journal of Christian Rural Concern* (Spring/Summer 2008), pp 15-17.

CHAPTER TWO

Evolution's Credit Crunch – Where Are We?

I will either go the whole hog with Darwin or, dispensing
with time and history altogether, hold not only the theory
of distinct species – but also of the creation of fossil-bearing
rocks.

John Henry Newman

Prominent in my hall, for my own inspiration and that of visitors,
are photographs of three photogenic men: John Henry Newman,
Teilhard de Chardin, and John Seymour, the latter as the most recent in colour. Nearby in Hastings, not far from 'the Hastings'
beds' loved by geologists, we currently commemorate Père
Teilhard's years studying theology, and paleontology, at Ore Place,
Hastings (1908-1912).[1] We also celebrated Charles Darwin's birth
and the publication of *The Origin of Species*. Teilhard admired both
Darwin and Newman, and read both at Ore Place where, like
Newman at Oxford, he studied 'the Cosmic Christ' of Saints Paul
and John and the Greek Church Fathers. While not engaged in
theology classes and study, Teilhard dug for fossils in the
Hastings beds and the cliffs and quarries of the Wealden clay.
Thanks in part to his reading of Newman, he said of his Ore Place
years that evolution 'haunted my mind like a tune'. John Seymour,
like Newman a devout convert to Catholicism which he described as 'the original church' was, like Jesus in his Nazareth
years, more 'hands on' than the scholarly Newman and Teilhard.
John championed 'the good life', partially self sufficient living,
and promoted William Cecil's wise advice to young men, 'Have a
little land around you.' The so-called 'credit crunch' and the en-
suing recession, combined with harbingers of climate change and

---

1. Norman Wildiers, *An Introduction to Teilhard de Chardin* (London:
Fontana, 1968), pp 180-181.

peaking oil production, and transition towns, have made John's partial self sufficiency important and timely. 'His writings', in the words of BBC's 'Countryfile', 'have influenced millions.' All three men loved and cherished their 'little land' around them, and through that part of earth, especially entrusted to them, the whole biosphere, described by Teilhard as 'that frail but superactive film of highly complex self-reproducing matter spread around the world', within which 'the noosphere' or human phenomenon, is 'the psychologically reflective human surface'.[2]

When standing before those three photographs in my hall, I realise we are, in Bernard of Chartres's metaphor, dwarfs standing on the shoulders of these – and many other – giants, including John Muir, Rachel Carson, Barbara Ward and F. W. Schumacher. Our challenge is with them to revere and rediscover in the whole evolving – and suffering – earth, 'the universal Christ', the human and living Jesus, in the depths of the cosmos and in the future. Of the three giants on my wall, only John Seymour confronted the frightening damage of anthropogenic climate change, which Newman and Teilhard knew only as a future possibility. The purpose of this chapter is to revisit evolution and to correlate evolution and planet earth's anthropogenic suffering, with contemporary Christian discipleship. To paraphrase the cartoon character Peanuts, we have met the church and it's us. We are Jesus Christ as community today when, in the words of former chief UK government scientist David King, 'People are removing the planet's biodiverse resources at a rate which is as fast if not faster than the world's last great extinction.'

Recently WWF issued a 'Living Planet' report to world governments. Chief Emeka Anyaoku, then chair of WWF, challenged not only leaders but all of us: 'Where is the collective action, the bold leadership, and the vision required to conserve the biodiversity of the planet? – I see very little of such passion.' 'Living Planet' notes that the earth's sustainable biocapacity, or living resources, is now a mere 2.1 hectares per person, of which the US and China alone consume nearly half. Worldwide the average *per capita* foot-

2. Pierre Teilhard de Chardin, *L'oeuvre scientifique*, N & K Schmitz-Moorman, eds (Olten: Waltec Verlaz, 1971), p 1480.

print is 2.7 hectares per person, in the UK it's 5.5 hectares per person, fifteenth in the world, just behind the Czech Republic. Still closer to home, to each of us, when we consider the importance of food security, is island Britain's limited biocapacity, which is a mere 1.6 hectares per person. Yet as just noted, our fossil fuel and 'trade' addicted footprint is an unsustainable 5.5. In contrast, the once resource rich US still has a biocapacity of 5 hectares per person, with a footprint of 9.4. In terms of homeland biocapacity and possible self sufficiency, therefore, Britain consumes even more than America and is, like America, a world class unsustainable mega-consumer. As developed world Christians, with those of other faiths, we need to reinterpret our heritage and evolutionary thought for a world suffering climate change and self-inflicted mass extinction by exceeding earth's biocapacity. Unfortunately the OECD and successive UK governments urge indefinite 'economic growth' despite our earth's finite and shrinking biocapacity. In wise contrast, Bishop James Jones of Liverpool says we need an 'economic atheism' in contrast to the creed of everlasting growth.

We can illustrate our current confusion of worldviews by a curious incident during one August Sunday Eucharist at Blackfriars Hall, Oxford. I was delighted to see my friend the late Herbert McCabe OP shuffle out as celebrant and preacher. As always, his sermon was stimulating, colourful, and challenging, this time particularly so, at least for some. For he remarked, almost in passing, that 'all prayer actually is petition'. At coffee after Mass and for at least the rest of that week, some mature women students were angered by that passing remark about prayer. In reflecting on that surprisingly heated reaction, I suspect Herbert was commenting provocatively on spiritualities in which God intervenes often, whereas we ourselves, like those women, are more familiar with the world which David Toolan describes:

> After all, the Unmoved Mover of Aristotle or the oriental despot who determines everything that happens down to the last twist and turn has never borne any resemblance to the God of the Bible. Ridding ourselves of these notions of omnipotence, then, should bring us closer to the biblical image of God –

to the God who lets creation develop in relative autonomy, who lets the world be, who renounces power and empties himself.[3]

Psychologised spiritualities are now popular with urban people alienated from the wider earth community and their own habitats, and ignorant of their local biosphere's limited capacity. Psychologised spiritualities, when engaged in exclusively, even obsessively, can and do lead urban people even further away from earth and into supposed personal depths. John Haught describes this contemporary phenomenon:

> Contemporary spirituality has instead typically undertaken the search for depth in terms of the personal 'inward journey', and the result, I believe, has been to prolong the modern sense of our isolation from the universe. If each fragmented psyche is borne afloat a limitless ocean of unconscious depth, it has seemed that the way to overcome our isolation is to embark on the long and painful pilgrimage into our own untapped inwardness. There and there alone, spiritual directors have told us, will we find the connection to meaning, or to God, that ordinary life in the outer world cannot provide. But meanwhile we have lost touch with the earth, the heavens and the abyss of evolutionary time.[4]

When individualism, consumerism and earth illiteracy combine, spiritualities of 'inner Sabbaths' and 'journeys within' attract many people. Hence their popularity in conference centres and summer schools. But they often are an indulgent distraction from the spirituality and 'God-talk' we now need – for ourselves, our earth, and the future – in our declining bioregions. Rather than 'inner journeys' we need spiritualities relevant to environmentalists and earth scientists. As Pope John Paul II said, in words still pertinent for our century, science 'can purify religion from error and superstition; religion can purify science from idolatry and false absolutes. Each can draw the other into a wider world, a

---

3. David Toolan SJ, *At Home in the Cosmos* (NY: Orbis, 2003), p 147.
4. John Haught, *Deeper Than Darwin* (Boulder: Westview, 2009), pp 34-35.

world in which both can flourish.'[5] The late Pope here points not inward but to holistic science which shares our concern – and responsibility – for the evolving biosphere, its climate and future. It is encouraging to see theologians and scientists in mutually respectful dialogue, some of whom, of which Teilhard is a notable forerunner, have some familiarity with another discipline, as we have just noticed in John Haught and the Jesuits at the Vatican Observatory.

Theology and 'Christ the Evolver'

In previous centuries most philosophy, theology, Christian ethics, and spirituality proceeded within a hierarchical, historical worldview, with people very much at the centre, if not 'the whole show' with a backdrop. We often imagined God as a Person analogous to human persons, towering above a vertical chain of beings. Even when we imagined God as 'Being Itself' or 'Letting Be', we still heard vertical echoes. Despite the rediscovery of literary forms and 'salvation history', it remained difficult to imagine the biosphere as other than fixed or static. In fact, all of us now must think and imagine – and believe and pray – humbly, in conversation with reliable theology and science. We must live and pray, conscious that we are within an evolving earth, dependent on God who is Holy Mystery. Charles Darwin and his neo-Darwinian disciples remind us of our humble origins. Humus and humility are from the same root. We are, it is true, God's image, with awesome responsibilities for the biosphere, but neo-Darwinians, with Mary Midgley, remind us, we 'are not just rather like animals; we *are* animals.'[6]

We are, moreover, thinking, responsible animals, hence our

---

5. Pope John Paul II, 'Message to the Director of the Vatican Observatory', in *Physics, Philosophy, and Theology: A Common Quest for Understanding,* eds Robert J. Russell, William R. Stoeger SJ, and George V. Coyne SJ (Rome: Vatican Observatory, 1997), M10, p 13.
6. Mary Midgley, *Beast and Man* (London: Routledge, 1995), p xxxiii; cf David Clough, 'The Anxiety of the Human Animal: Martin Luther on Non-human Animals and Human Animality', in Celia Deane-Drummond and David Clough, eds, *Creaturely Theology, On God, Humans and Other Animals* (London: SCM, 2009), pp 41-61.

honoured classification '*homo sapiens*'. In our frail biosphere, we are relative newcomers. The friendly hedgehogs, who occasionally visit my garden and reduce invertebrate parasites, have been around for almost 15 million years longer than woolly mammoths and sabre toothed tigers. We human come-latelys seem to have arrived in Africa a mere 150,000 years ago, evolving from our smaller ancestor *homo erectus* who had been around for a mere 2 million years. Always 'upwardly mobile', sixty thousand years ago we settled in Europe and Asia, 50,000 years ago we were in Australia, and 13,000 years ago, well before Columbus, our ancestors discovered America. In brief, when we look at the discoveries of paleontology and geology, the stories of an immediate human creation appear as what they were meant to be, imaginative not scientific. So mysterious is evolution, its adaptations, selections, survivals, and extinctions that we need respectful reticence when talking about creation. People are intuitively conscious of relatedness, especially a deep relatedness to Holy Mystery that transcends other relationships, a Holy Presence within and beyond the cosmos, in the depths of and yet beyond creation. That deep relatedness is to God who, as Karl Rahner said so well, is 'ineffable Darkness', 'Holy Mystery', beyond thought and words, 'past all grasp God', with whose grandeur the world is charged. For Charles Darwin himself, as for Gerard Manley Hopkins, God was indeed 'past all grasp' but that does not mean that Darwin was an atheist. Shortly before he died, Darwin wrote in a letter to John Fordyce,

> It seems to me absurd to doubt that a man may be an ardent Theist and an evolutionist … In my most extreme fluctuations I have never been an atheist in the sense of denying the existence of a God. I think that generally (and more and more so as I grow older) but not always, that an agnostic would be the most correct description of my state of mind.[7]

God's self-disclosure, whether 'natural' as in deep human experience of relatedness or 'supernatural' as in revelation, is God's disclosure in mystery. We need to recover our apophatic or nega-

---

7. Darwin Correspondence Project Database. http://www.darwinproject
.ac.uk/entry-12041

tive tradition, wherein we are reticent and hesitant in what we say about Holy Mystery, about creation's origins, and about our own place within the created evolving biosphere. And we must integrate evolution with our theology, spirituality, worship, and practice. As John Haught says:

> Theology's typical slighting of evolution is symptomatic of a lack of courage in religious instruction and theological imagination. To us, it is the signal of a lost opportunity for spiritual, theological and intellectual growth. We are convinced that a serious encounter of theology with contemporary versions of evolutionary science may not only enrich our understanding of the universe but also revitalise our sense of divine providence. If theology is to flourish within contemporary intellectual culture, our understanding of how God cares for the universe requires fresh expression in evolutionary terms.[8]

To say earth is God's creation is not to describe beginnings 'out of nothing', still less a 'Big Bang', but to profess earth's contingency, or utter dependence on God. Every instant, including and beyond all beginning, is creation. Nicholas Lash observes, 'The recognition of contingency, what Schleiermacher called the sense of absolute dependence, may (like vertigo) be intermittently exhilarating, but its more lasting moods lie somewhere between sheer mind-stopping awe and stark terror.'[9] We should add that creation as contingent is unfinished. Intrinsic to our faith and hope is Christ's return. Creation has a future (and present) in him, even in entropy. Our faith and hope is not that God will make a new thing, but 'all things new' (Rev 21:5), including plant and animal companions we have known and loved here.

What then about 'the fall'? Why are contingent humans, of all earth creatures, the most perverse and deadly? Why do we extinguish other species, and threaten the stability of the biosphere with climate change? Why did our first ancestors choose death? Or did they? We are beginning to learn, as Rowan Williams tried to ex-

---

8. Haught, *Deeper Than Darwin*, p 78.
9. Nicholas Lash, *Believing Three Ways in One God, A Reading of the Apostles Creed* (South Bend: Notre Dame Press, 1993), p 39.

plain to Richard Dawkins, that the Bible is 'full of pictures', of poetry and literary forms, that the Bible appeals to the imagination. Despite fundamentalist efforts to portray an original 'fall' of a man and a woman, the creation story and Paul's reference to it are neither history nor science, but more. They teach through literature. The beautiful creation accounts denote human moral evil, or sin and its propensity, as inherent in the human condition. Humans are frail, finite, and mortal, as are all our fellow earth creatures. People (Adam) are soil creatures, from the soil, (*adamah*). We and our fellow creatures of the soil community, even as suffering, competitive, selective, and extinctive, are interconnected (*juntos*). Far from being the effect of a primordial fall, death is the font of life. Arthur Peacocke, a theologically informed scientist aware of scripture's appeal to Wordsworth's 'wonderful world of eye and ear', in his study of evolution recognised the Bible as literature:

> Biological death can no longer be regarded as in any way the consequences of anything human beings might have been supposed to have done in the past, for evolutionary history shows it to be the very means whereby they appear, and so, for the theist, are created by God. The traditional interpretation of the third chapter of Genesis that there was a historical 'Fall', an action by our human progenitors that is the explanation of biological death, has to be rejected ... There was no golden age, no perfect past, no individual 'Adam' or 'Eve' from whom all human beings have descended and declined and who were perfect in their relationships and behaviour.[10]

In the natural world, therefore, the whole earth community, including *homo sapiens*, endures suffering from birth and, as we just noticed, the death from which flows life. The point I am making is that the Bible pictures poetically what evolution also unfolds: namely, that all earth creatures are included in 'the fall', that is, we all suffer together, especially through human moral evil, just as we are all 'very good' together (Gen 1:31; 3:16-19). Within

10. Arthur Peacocke, *Theology for a Scientific Age. Being and Becoming – Natural, Divine and Human* (Oxford: Blackwell, 1947), pp 222-223.

the earth community humans have unique tendencies to greed and exploitation, and unique powers and responsibilities. Paul's famous description of shared suffering and hope has never been more relevant. This is not to suggest that Paul was aware of evolution as we know it, but that he was certainly aware, and teaches, that people and the rest of the earth community are interconnected and interdependent, that other creatures suffer when we falter, and that they 'groan' in anticipation of our 'revelation' as God's sons, in the better future we share (Rom 8:19-23).

God Talk

Christians have always struggled to talk reverently and precisely about ineffable Holy Mystery. The first five centuries of Christian history, when a nascent theology developed in the light of Jesus' resurrection and in the power of God's living Spirit, were largely engaged in finding ways to talk about God, especially God's action in Jesus. For God is one, but God is three Persons in one nature, the Word and Spirit consubstantial (of one nature) with the Father. God's Word, from the moment of incarnation in Jesus, is God in human flesh, incarnate within the earth community. Mary is therefore '*theotokos*', the mother bearer of God. These early precisions do not mean 'God-talk', to borrow the title of John Macquarrie's book, is forever set in stone. On the contrary, in early centuries as now in every century, Christians reticently re-fine our thought and language about God – for ourselves and for those to whom we preach in deed and word. As Christopher Southgate, impressed by Orthodox reticence, says, 'Whatever we seek to say of God is always lamentably partial and inadequate, at its best fractionally better than silence.'[11]

Our ancestors were challenged by the discoveries of their own times, such as whole new continents and people, and by the extent of physical and moral evil. So are we challenged by discoveries of the apparent disorder of evolution and its inherent suffering, compounded since the arrival of our species by horrendous moral evils such as anthropogenic climate change, sea pollution, and confiscation of heritage seeds. Richard Dawkins notices the inher-

---

11. Southgate, *The Groaning of Creation*, p 55.

ent suffering in the universe, 'The universe we observe has precisely the properties we would expect if there is, at bottom, no design, no purpose, no evil, and no good, nothing but blind pitiless indifference.'[12] We may remind ourselves of the 98% of species now extinct, and the suffering we observe everywhere around us – including, beyond Dawkins, the creatures deprived of habitats by unnecessary roads, runways, carparks, and slabbed urban gardens – the suffering wrought by 'complexity conscious' humanity through wars, deforestation, pollution, extinction, unsustainable procreation and mass urbanisation. Even the fittest survivors in our evolving biosphere, as we are reminded in wars, famines, and intensive care units, suffer grievously. Suffering and death, extinction and moral evil perplexed our ancestors no less than ourselves. Even in a neater neo-Platonic age they lived faithfully with mystery, for them too God was 'ineffable Darkness'. In continuity with and fidelity to them we must, for our very different and evolutionary context, reinterpret and re-express their faith, their God-talk. We need, in Jean Danielou's wonderful expression to 're-interrogate' the sources of their faith and ours for a secularising world which is also the world of the rediscovery of 'faiths', the contemporary world in which humanity is using annually about a third more resources than earth can replenish, the world of biotechnology, deforestation, glacier melting, urbanisation, reality avoiding politicians and media, and nuclear power. The commission of the risen Jesus, relayed poetically to us by Matthew, still stands: our mission is to teach all nations (Mt 28:19f).

I submit that a key biblical text for our time is the hymn incorporated by the first Christian writer, Paul of Tarsus, in his letter to the Philippians, about Holy Mystery as self-emptying, even suffering, in Jesus 'who, though he was in the form of God, did not count equality with God a thing to be grasped, but emptied himself, taking the form of a servant' (Phil 2:6-7). In other words, God of the 'Big Bang', of biospheric evolution, of entropy, of the second law of thermodynamics, and of the terminal dying of the sun and earth, does not interfere or choose always to be Almighty. Still less

12. Richard Dawkins, *River Out of Eden, A Darwinian View of Life* (London: Phoenix, 2001), p 133.

does God, in Jesus, intervene in detail in our daily lives. Rather, we require a theology and spirituality for our evolving biosphere, wasted by anthropogenic climate disruption and positive feedback, a biosphere in which God remains present and all powerful, but self-emptying, our God who suffered and died in Jesus. In Dietrich Bonhoeffer's words, 'God allows himself to be pushed out of the world and onto the cross. Only a suffering God can help.' Suffering raises the question of God in evolution's travail. Does God co-suffer with us and with our myriad fellow creatures, all of whom eventually fail, age and die, and millions of whom are already extinct including, let us remember, micro-organisms even smaller than earthworms and slugs?

The Suffering of Evolution

Some contemporary thinkers, including the late Arthur Peacocke and now Christopher Southgate, argue that God 'suffers' with God's suffering creatures. If by God's co-suffering we mean presence, compassion, love, care, promise of the kingdom and a blessed future, I agree. The hypothesis of God in process, however, effected by and at least analogously suffering with suffering creatures, though consoling, is not always convincing. To talk about God in process and suffering may venture to say too much about Holy Mystery. On the other hand if by co-suffering we mean attentive loving solidarity, caring presence which fills what would be the void of absence, I can agree that God 'co-suffers' with his creatures. In Southgate's words,

> God's suffering presence is just that, presence, of the most profoundly attentive and loving sort, a solidarity that at some deep level takes away the aloneness of the suffering creature's experience. Again this is necessarily an anthropomorphic guess, but both acute and chronic suffering must isolate the creature, and may lead to what (for humans at least) is one of the most terrible of all experiences, that of dying alone, with no connection to care or fellow-feeling of any sort. God's presence to and solidarity with the suffering creature, then, is an important ingredient in an evolutionary theodicy.[13]

13. Southgate, *The Groaning of Creation*, pp 52-53.

Describing the suffering inherent in evolution, Jay McDaniel and Holmes Royston III illustrate evolution's losers by the white pelican 'insurance chick'. These lovely and symbiotic creatures have survived and served the biosphere for 30 million years. Female white pelicans often produce not just one but two sibling chicks. The younger is a back-up or standby 'insurance chick' which gets neglected at the rim of the nest where it is easily pushed out by its well fed sibling. The purpose of these frail, starved, unloved creatures is to insure the survival of their species, in which they have succeeded for millions of years. For if the leader fledgling sickens and dies the insurance chick gets fed and nurtured and becomes cock of the nest, like a Chinese 'little emperor'. Certainly this adaptive survival mechanism has succeeded for the pelican species. But what about the rejected chicks? When they die – as they soon do – their bodies in neo-scholastic jargon are reduced to the potency of the matter, they continue to serve the biosphere even as disintegrating and decaying within the soil – but what about them as individual chicks? They too, in Gerard Manley Hopkins' words, have 'selved', they too can or could say, 'What I am is me, for that I came', they too are like the sparrows that fall or get sold in the market place. God is present and cares and, most important, is future for them too. In this sense I agree that God co-suffers with white pelican insurance chicks, fallen sparrows, and starving people.

When scripture says God found all that he had made 'very good', this includes creation's future when all will be indeed very good. Meanwhile there remain struggle, chance, danger, famine, adaptation, selection, extinction and survival of species. Complex, conscious, rational creatures – that's us – have evolved. We now struggle to 'conquer' nature – we pollute, overpopulate, strip and ravage the biosphere, damage climate, and threaten the very survival of life on earth as relatively recently evolved humans have known it. Some argue that this disorderly, chaotic, chancy, competitive, and selective evolution is 'the only way' God could allow human creatures to evolve.[14] That this is the way human mammals have evolved is uncontroversial. But it may be rather too

---

14. Ibid., p 48.

confident in human investigative and analytic capacities to say it is 'the only way'. I find evolution and its suffering mysteries as I do the possibly terminal damage involved in what humans are now doing to the planet. Almost everywhere I look in the UK men (and many women) are uncaringly destroying habitats, biosystems, and fellow creatures for what is called 'economic growth', 'development', 'regeneration', and 'progress', or simply enjoyment. As Thomas Berry said, it seems as if humans contain a repressed rage against the restraints under which life on earth is granted. The whole evolving earth community, including people themselves, suffer from this rage. And why the self-emptying and personal God permits evil and suffering remains mystery. The earth community also suffers from physical evil independent of human agency. Television presenter and Operation Noah campaign strategist, Mark Dowd, produced a two hour documentary, repeated at its fifth anniversary on God and the 2004 tsunami. Although he interviewed representatives of several other faiths and of various Christian perspectives, Dowd was most impressed by the Jesuits at the Vatican Observatory. In Jesus, our Creator is the self-emptying God. The blessing of creation includes the cross. I prefer hesitation and reticence before this mystery – and the mystery of human death – to 'the only way' hypothesis. Neil Messer observes:

> We can infer that in some sense the non-human creation needs saving, whether because it is directly affected by human sin (as the biosphere of planet earth is, in obvious and serious ways) or because in some other way it is 'fallen', flawed or diverted from God's good purposes for it. Thus Paul can write that the creation is 'subjected to futility' and that the saving work of God centred in Christ extends to the liberation of creation from its 'bondage to decay' (Rom 8:18-24). Again, considerable reticence is in order as to the nature of this futility and the manner of this liberation: there is a great deal that we do not, and perhaps cannot, know, and that may be God's concern but none of ours.[15]

15. Neil Messer, *Selfish Genes and Christian Ethics* (London: SCM Press, 2007), p 214.

We noticed that God 'co-suffers' with God's creatures in his compassionate, sustaining presence. Moreover, God suffers with and for us in his self-emptying even unto death of the most heinous, unsedated kind, in the passion and cross of the suffering and dying Jesus. We sometimes fail to notice that Jesus also, and literally, suffered all the endemic frailties of the human condition during his life on earth. These sufferings are part of our healing. Furthermore, in his resurrection Jesus begins – is the 'first fruits' – of the long anticipated future of evolution. Jesus risen, in Raymond E. Brown's words, is the beginning of the future of the earth. We may recall Chardin, 'in your own incarnation, my God, the immense host which is the universe is incarnate'. In Jesus, incarnate and risen, all things are reconciled, redeemed, included in evolution's future. It would be difficult to improve on the Pauline hymn so loved by Teilhard, 'For in him all the fullness of God was pleased to dwell, and through him to reconcile to himself all things, whether on earth or in heaven, making peace by the blood of his cross' (Col 1:20).

All Things Mean All

Those small words 'all things' (*ta panta*) encompass a mind stretching reality and are not without controversy. The Bible is not an academic treatise; nor does it teach modern science. It does, however, as we noted, teach through the imaginative power, 'the wonderful world of eye and ear'. Therefore, by 'all' I suggest the Bible implies and connotes literally all creatures. All earth, and cosmic, suffering creation is included, reconciled, redeemed, saved, loved forever, in the all embracing arms of Jesus' self-bestowal and acceptance by the Father in the Holy Spirit. It has been suggested that by 'all' the New Testament means all conscious or at least highly evolved beings, or beings we have known in this life, but not inclusively all. On the contrary, it teaches through implication, connotation, and imagination that even micro-organisms that we have never known, or that are now extinct, and everything that preceded anthropogenesis, the arrival of our species, are included in the all embracing love of God through Jesus. That 'all things' includes even those unknown creatures poignantly described by Mikhail Gorbachev, which were 'buried' after Chernobyl. A man involved in the initial clean-up after the catastrophe was moved almost to tears by what he found – and had to bury!

> Of course someone who considers soil to be our 'bread-giver' will find it hard to come to terms with the thought of 'interring' it. But this man was especially surprised at the multitude of insects entirely unknown to him which he found living in that ground: 'Living layers of earth … with beetles, spiders, worms in them … I didn't know their names, I had no idea what they were called … They were just beetles and spiders. Ants. Large and small ones, yellow and black. So colourful. In a lyric poem I once read of animals being little tribes on their own account. I killed them by the dozen, by the hundred, by the thousand without even knowing their names. I destroyed their dwellings. Their secrets. I buried … and buried…'[16]

We touch mystery here, but I repeat that 'all' embraces literally all beings that have lived, including those who preceded us on this planet or were never known, or never will be known by our species, and all those who *will* live. Even if the universe ends in a crunch or in heat, even if energy necessarily dissipates, all creation will be mysteriously transformed and healed and alive again in Jesus risen. God loves and is now present in all and each creature. This presence, even here in this evolving earth is not pantheism. God remains God, transcendent and wholly Other, as well as present.

Karl Rahner, R. E. Brown, and numerous contemporary theologians and spiritual writers, like Teilhard, also speak of Christ present or immanent within the earth. At a recent theology conference at Cambridge, two young American theologians told me that, as evangelicals, they were troubled by the presence of 'the universal Christ', Christ risen within the cosmos. My two young colleagues said they find this teaching difficult to comprehend, and to communicate, especially in the pulpit. Their commitment

---

16. Mikhail Gorbachev, *Manifesto for the Earth, Action Now for Peace, Global Justice and a Sustainable Future* (Forest Row: Clairview, 2006), pp 43-44.

and pastoral zeal touched and still challenges me. I reminded them, for example, of Père Teilhard's own reflection on the same Pauline letters which they love, and of his conclusion that 'in your own incarnation, my God, the immense host which is the universe is made incarnate.' We agreed on the caution and care Christian outreach needs in speaking of Holy Mystery, nowhere more so than in eschatology, or speaking of the future. Karl Rahner recalled an important warning of the medieval philosopher Nicholas of Cusa (d. 1464) – to preserve the *docta ignorantia futuri* (the learned unknown of the future). Our task, Rahner insisted, is to resist closure, to recognise there is and remains mystery.[17] Scripture remains helpful, for it teaches the inclusion of all creation in God's future, notably in Isaian texts and in Paul, Col 1:15f; Eph 1:9-10, and in Rev 21:5 where, significantly, God says not that he will make a new thing, but *all things* new. Reflecting on these and other texts, Denis Edwards combines the cautious hesitation we have endorsed with the attestation that all creatures mysteriously are included in everlasting life in God,

> I have been proposing that each creature, each little sparrow, is known and loved by God, is eternally inscribed in God by the Holy Spirit, participates in redemption in Christ, and is eternally held and treasured in the life of the Trinity. The diverse range of creatures that springs from the abundance of this divine communion finds redemption in being taken up eternally into this communion. Because God relates to each creature on its own terms, final fulfillment will fit the nature of each creature. There is every reason to believe that individual creatures will find their proper redemption in the divine communion in a way that we cannot fully articulate.[18]

Future reconciliation, the eschaton, if it is to be truly paradise, as Fr Peter Doodes has observed, will include the pets we have known, loved, and bonded with here. Bereavement of animal

---

17. Karl Rahner, 'The Question of the Future', *Theological Investigations*, Vol 12 (London: Darton Longman & Todd, 1974), pp 181-201.
18. Denis Edwards, *Ecology at the Heart of Faith* (Marynoll: Orbis, NY), 2006, p 98.

friends without hope in their future would be pitiless. My own animal friends with whom I have shared love and life include four peke companions here in Britain: by name, Joseph, Paulinus, Bertha, and Mildred. Each is an individual, each, that is, is a peke, each 'selves', is unique and says 'what I am is me', each lives in my memory, my heart, and in the cosmos, in Wordsworth's apposite words, 'rolled round in earth's diurnal course, with rocks and stones and trees'. Innocent, trusting, sinless, like us they suffer decline and death. Even in death they remain with us by remaining within earth's diurnal course. Even when we move house and garden where they are buried, they accompany us in the cosmos. John Wesley pondered the mystery of innocent suffering, as have we, and concluded, as do we, that 'there would be a plausible objection against that justice of God, in suffering numberless creatures that had never sinned to be so severely punished'. Having studied the scriptures, as have we, Wesley concluded, 'the objection vanishes away if we consider that something better after death awaits for these creatures also; and they likewise shall one day be delivered from the bondage to corruption and shall then receive an ample amends for all their suffering.'[19] It is abundantly clear from our experience, and taught by the Bible, that 'all things' are affected by our actions, including our 'fall' or innate tendency to greed and rebellion against God's and the earth's restraints. They also share our future healing (Rom 8:19-23). For so interconnected are we earth creatures that in John Muir's famous – and ecologically and theologically perceptive – remark, 'when we try to pick out anything by itself, we find it hitched to everything else in the universe.'

God's kingdom is ahead. We live not in fulfillment, but in hope for ourselves and other creatures, including the interred microbes and ants of Chernobyl, and our own pets and garden birds. Christian hope is active hope in God's kingdom and the return of Christ. Neil Messer notes of our active hope:

We cannot and need not perfect or save the world by our own

---

19. John Wesley, 'The General Deliverance', in *Sermons on Several Occasions*, Vol II (London: J. Kershaw, 1825), pp 121-132.

efforts; this 'ultimate' work is God's, not ours. But it leaves us the 'penultimate' responsibility of acting in the world so as to 'shape the future', or to improve the world and the conditions of human life in it. Not to do so would be a refusal of our vocation and a betrayal of our responsibility that would perpetuate the distortion of our relations with God, one another and the world.[20]

Matthew's Jesus includes in the Sermon on the Mount the wise warning 'Do not be anxious about tomorrow, for tomorrow will be anxious for itself. Let the day's own trouble be sufficient for the day' (Mt 6:34). That last sentence reminds us that if Christian hope is active, we have work to do which is not often easy. We will die with 'unfinished business'. Jesus had an affinity with the Isaian teachings which point to the future and, as we have noticed, include our fellow creatures. Inspiring for our time of industrial culture's induced climate change, overpopulation and diminishing and tainted aquifers, are Isaiah's hopeful words about God's provision of life-giving water both for his people and for other sensate creatures (Is 43:19-21). Yet perversely in this our nuclear and biotechnical and motorised time, we forget earth's restraints. Instead of serving God and the earth community as co-creators and co-sufferers in preparation for the kingdom, we destroy earth's creatures from forests to micro-organisms, to aquifers and climate. John Haught warns, 'Creation carries in its present perishable glory the seeds of a final eschatological flowering. Hence, by allowing the embryonic future to perish now at the hands of our own ecological carelessness and selfishness we not only violate nature's sacramental bearing but also turn away from the promise that lies embedded in all of creation.'[21]

As Christians our responsibility is to restore co-operative symbiosis within the evolving biosphere. Christopher Jamieson suggests we contribute our tradition of the moral virtues: prudence, justice, fortitude and temperance, grounded in the theo-

---

20. Messer, *Selfish Genes and Christian Ethics*, pp 210-211.
21. John Haught, *God AfterDarwin, A Theology of Evolution* (Boulder: Westminster Press, 2000), p 151.

logical virtues of faith, hope and charity.[22] Living the virtues we preach and prepare for God's kingdom. We serve in our evolving biosphere which, scientists assure us, will continue, despite human damage even without our species. Our particular mission, therefore, is to assist people and earth to evolve in a mutually supportive way with its human inhabitants.

Teilhard de Chardin
When considering the Christian interpretation of and response to evolution, we stand beside and on the shoulders of Pierre Teilhard de Chardin (1886-1955). Teilhard lived, at least where Christian theology and social teaching is concerned, a generation ahead of his time. Persons ahead of their time inevitably draw some inferences and conclusions which later need refinement. Teilhard was no exception. For an innovator lives within a culture of received knowledge, wisdom and experience of contemporaries, some of whom will later criticise and refine his thoughts, while developing his insights and standing on his shoulders. Teilhard seemed to realise this himself. In a late and major publication, he insisted:

> I am not exaggerating in the least. The more deeply science plumbs the past of our humanity, the more clearly does it see that humanity, as a species, conforms to the rhythm and the rules that marked each new offshoot on the tree of life before the advent of mankind. Thus we are logically obliged to pursue the subject to its conclusion. Since *Homo Sapiens* is at birth so similar to the other *phyla*, let us stop being surprised if, as with all living groups, the fragile secrets of his earliest origins give our science the slip; and let us henceforward forbear to force and falsify this natural condition with clumsy questionings.[23]

Teilhard learned to love the natural world as a boy in the hills

---

22. Christopher Jamieson, 'Might of Metaphysics', *The Tablet* (15 November 2008), pp 9-10.
23. Pierre Teilhard de Chardin, *The Phenomenon of Man* (NY: Harper & Row, 1959), p 185.

and fields around his family home in the Auvergne, especially with his naturalist father. That love of rocks, flora, and fauna persisted all his life, and deepened in Jesuit years at Aix, Jersey, Cairo, Hastings, Paris, China, and, finally, amid the stones and varied birds and fauna of New York's Central Park. Teilhard was not born an evolutionist. Far from it. His youthful spirituality and philosophy tended to a low, even dualist view of matter. Yet he loved walking and discovering the shale and fossils of Jersey, where he studied philosophy, and in Cairo where he taught as a scholastic (Jesuit student). It was especially when studying theology at Ore Place, Hastings, at the dawn of French *nouvelle theologie* that he discovered evolution which, he said, 'haunted my mind like a tune'. Teilhard was at Ore Place from 1908-1912, where his superiors allowed him in his free time to explore 'the cliffs and quarries of the Wealden clay which held the stones I was seeking.' There he read Charles Darwin, and John Henry Newman's *Essay on the Development of Doctrine*, and was influenced by the thrust if not all the details of Henri Bergson's *L'Evolution Creatrice*. Teachers and peers in a student's undergraduate years are an influence that remain all one's life. Teilhard was no exception. Among his distinguished professors were Léonce de Grandmaison, and Père de Genouillac. Fellow scholastics included the brilliant and tragically short lived Pierre Rousselet, Joseph Huby, Jules Lebreton, August Valensin, and Felix Pelletier, a fellow fossil seeker in the 'Hastings beds' and Wealden clay, and Auguste Decisier, destined to become Teilhard's provincial and, as one who knew him and the mystical depth of his thought, a lifelong friend and defender.[24]

It was especially at Ore Place that Teilhard pondered 'the cosmic Christ' of Saints John and Paul and the Greek fathers. The Pauline hymns and the cosmic inclusion of the risen Christ and his Sacred Heart, 'the universal Christ', thenceforth ran like a thread through all Teilhard's thought and writings. His younger fellow Jesuit and friend, Henri de Lubac, who later became Teilhard's biographer and defender, was an advisor to the Cardinal of Cracow, later Pope John Paul II, at Vatican II. The Polish Pope, an

24. Robert Speaght, *Teilhard de Chardin, a Biography* (London: Wm Clowes and Sons, 1967), pp 36-37.

admirer of Teilhard, assimilated Teilhard's mystical insight of a 'cosmic nature' in Christ. Of Teilhard's rootedness in the tradition de Lubac notes:

> He knew that, in the main lines of his thought, he had been faithful to St Paul and St John, and there are many competent exegetes today who would be inclined to agree with him. He felt, too, that he was carrying on the speculative effort of the Greek Fathers, in particular St Irenaeus and St Gregory of Nyssa, to whom he more than once alludes, though in a general and rather inexact way. He believed also that his concept of Christ the evolver should have the effect of 'giving traditional Christianity a new reinforcement of up-to-dateness and vitality'. We may wonder, too, how far he realised that he was thus, in a new context conditioned by new scientific advances, forging a more exact bond with an ancient tradition running through so many long centuries.[25]

Teilhard was not a professional theologian, but a paleontologist, a mystic, poet, spiritual writer, and synthesiser of theological and spiritual insights with science. He attempted to relate his theological discoveries at Ore Place to Ignatian spirituality, and to devotion to the personal, universal Christ, with his human Sacred Heart at the centre of the cosmos, and in 'all things'. These in turn he attempted to synthesise with science and evolution. His original, unique, and sometimes controversial insights still inspire many in our time of climate change and what President Obama calls 'a planet in peril'. Teilhard tended to be optimistic in temperament and a believer in 'progress', including development in evolution:

> So as to overcome the improbability of arrangements leading to units of ever increasing complexity, the involuting universe, considered in its pre-reflective zones, proceeds step by step by dint of billion-fold trial and error. It is this process of groping, combined with the two-fold mechanism of reproduction and heredity (allowing the hoarding and the additive improve-

---

25. Henri de Lubac, *Teilhard de Chardin, The Man and His Meaning* (NY: Burns and Oates, 1967), pp 54-55.

ment of favourable combinations obtained, without the diminution, indeed with the increase, of the number of individuals engaged), which gives rise to the extraordinary assemblage of living stems forming what I have called the tree of life.[26]

'All things cohere in him', *omnia in ipso constant*, was Teilhard's empowering mystical vision from his study of scripture and the Greek Fathers at Ore Place. He searched in the fossil record for 'the future of man'. He said he searched the past to discover the future. Combining paleontology with spirituality he called the future consummation and attraction 'the Omega Point', convergence in the universal Christ of the future, who is also 'Christ the evolver'. F. LeRon Shults of Agder University, Norway, comments, cautiously, 'this radical integration of the doctrine of the *parousia* into an all-embracing interpretation of the evolution of the universe has had its detractors, but it remains one of the most significant attempts to articulate the Christian experience of the presence of Christ in a way that coheres with big bang cosmology.'[27] It is sometimes objected, including by sympathetic Christians, that evolution does not develop nor progress, but is blind, wasteful, extinctive, replete with adaptation for survival of the fittest. Many, while sympathetic to Teilhard's attempts at synthesis, have criticised his scheme of 'complexity consciousness', unification, and development in evolution as foreign to Darwin and neo-Darwinism, and indeed modern environmentalism. For Teilhard thought the human presence or 'noosphere', in its development and unification of different cultures, drove evolution forward:

> According to my point of view, culturation is nothing but a 'hominised' form of speciation or, to express the same thing differently, cultural units are for the noosphere the mere equivalent and the true successors of zoological species in the biosphere. True successors, we insist. And how much better fitted than their predecessors to satisfy the new requisites of an advanced type of evolution![28]

26. Chardin, *Phenomenon of Man*, pp 301-302.
27. F. LeRon Shults, *Christology and Science* (Aldershot: Ashgate Publishing, 2008), p 241.
28. Chardin, *L'oeuvre scientifique*, p 4585.

Teilhard's mystical vision still fascinates us. For despite entropy and the near terminal human abuse of the living biosphere, the Christian hope is that, in Teilhard's words, 'the universal Christ', will transform the earth and make 'all things new' (Rev 21:5). Much is made, rightly, of the fact that Teilhard died some years before Rachel Carson's *Silent Spring* and the growth of environmentalism. And, we should add, the 1992 Rio Earth summit, when despite unprecedented media coverage, urbanising peoples everywhere chose denial rather than admission of 'the restraints under which life is granted'. While we may regret Teilhard's empathy with the 20th century progress myth and his developmental view of evolution, we should also notice his elderly awareness of human earth abuse. In a lecture to the Jesuit community at Fordham he described the overpopulation in China, and the desirability of '*quale non quantum*' by which he meant quality of life with procreative restraint. Also in New York, shortly before his death, he described overpopulation and its concomitant depletion of bio-resources as 'a dangerous and distressing situation, inasmuch as it presents us with a whole world of vital problems: food supplies, health, the easing of the nervous strain suffered by a vast number of human beings brought into such close proximity.'[29] Today we might add biodiversity loss and surface and subterranean water depletion, about which the United Nations met in 1996, 2000 and 2008.

What he had witnessed of modern human impact, while studying 'continental paleontology' in China moved Chardin. He was before his time in his awareness of deforestation and its damaging effects on the biosphere. He regretted 'The incredible negligence of the Chinese, who are destroying and wasting all their forests without seeming to suspect that they are helping to feed the floods and to destroy their fields.'[30] He noticed the early destruction of Vietnam forests for rubber plantations, a forerunner of forest demolition for palm oil, soya, cattle ranching, and even

29. Pierre Teilhard de Chardin, *The Activation of Energy* (NY: Harcourt Brace Jovanovich, 1971), p 212.

30. Pierre Teilhard de Chardin, *Letters to Two Friends* (Cleveland: World Publishing, 1969), p 39.

biofuels. Here however his controversial belief in progress breaks through:

> What impressed me even more than the luxuriance of the vegetable and animal life in these regions is the destructive and assimilative power of Man. Already the savages (the Mois) are fairly skilled in burning the bush. But before the Europeans with their roads and railroads the forest is literally melting. It is rubber, above all, which threatens to replace everything. Once I would have been furious and inconsolable at the sight of this devastation or conquest. Now I think I understand that we are witnessing the establishment of a new Zone of Life around the earth, and that it would be absurd to regret the disappearance of an old envelope which must fall.[31]

Teilhard opposed hunting. He anticipated widespread vegetarianism, as in the first Genesis creation story, within his progressive 'noosphere' wherein (globalised) humans will 'build the earth':

> Getting back to the respect for life, we find ourselves, of course, in a natural system in which the mutual destruction of living things seems to be a condition of equilibrium and survival. But what is true of the animal world may perhaps diminish progressively with the establishment of the human sphere: a decline in useless destruction and, as Vernadsky predicts, the discovery of nourishment drawn from the inorganic.[32]

The last surviving member of a large loving family, Teilhard suffered the deaths of parents and siblings. He had also served as a stretcher bearer in the trenches shortly after leaving theological studies at Ore Place. He was keenly conscious, especially in his frail final years, of the suffering inherent in the human phenomenon, including decline, old age and depression, from which he too suffered in his last years. Teilhard died and was buried in New York, almost a virtual exile, far from his native Auvergne and adopted 'second home' in Paris. Although death brings new

---

31. Ibid., p 27.
32. Ibid., p 42.

life on earth, death brings suffering to the individual. In Teilhard's own words:

> If by chance we escape, to a greater or lesser extent, the critical forms of these assaults from without which appear deep within us and irresistibly destroy the strength, the light, and the love by which we live, there still remains that slow, essential deterioration which we cannot escape: old age little by little robbing us of ourselves and pushing us on toward the end. Time, which postpones possession, time which tears us away from enjoyment, time which condemns us all to death.[33]

Despite failing health, Teilhard remained an optimist even in his declining years in New York, where he delighted in daily 'constitutional' walks enjoying the rocks, flora and fauna of Central Park. Significantly, however, and not always noticed, he added in 1948, seven years before his death, an appendix to *The Phenomenon of Man* which reveals his realistic awareness of human greed and aggression. He even considered the neo-Augustinian theory then prevalent in France – and influential even in the Vatican – about an historical primordial stumble,

> Is it really sure that, for an eye trained and sensitised by light other than that of pure science, the quantity and the malice of evil *hic et nunc*, spread throughout the world, does not betray a certain excess, inexplicable to our reason, if to the normal effect of evolution is not added the extraordinary effect of some catastrophe or primordial deviation?[34]

Conclusion

Teilhard's death in New York was consistent with his life, indeed a new beginning. He had always hoped to die at Easter, which he did, suddenly, on Easter Sunday 1955, having celebrated the eucharist of the resurrection in the morning. He was buried, as New York Jesuits then were, in the cemetery at Poughkeepsie, appropriately an aboriginal name, on the Hudson river. He remains

---

33. Pierre Teilhard de Chardin, *The Divine Milieu: An Essay on the Interior Life* (London: Collins / Fontana, 1963), pp 58-60.
34. Chardin, Appendix, *Phenomenon of Man*, p 311.

there still with his Jesuit brethren, but also with his parents, siblings and friends (and my own – and my pets) 'rolled round in
earth's diurnal course', with all things in 'the universal Christ', in
our evolving biosphere. As he said in a final '*pensée*', 'in place of
the undefined point of convergence required as term for this evolution it is the clearly defined personal reality of the incarnate
Word that is made manifest to us and established for us as
our objective, that Word "in whom all things subsist".'[35]

Teilhard's continuing attraction was evidenced when in
September 2008, the anniversary of his arrival at Ore Place,
Hastings District Council erected a plaque at the entrance of Ore
Place, now a housing estate, commemorating Teilhard's four
years there. I attended the unveiling ceremony at which the Chair
of Hastings District Council, and Fr Billy Hewett SJ, of Campion
Hall, Oxford, spoke briefly. Hewett added a characteristic quote
of Teilhard, rooted in his years of study at Ore Place, in which he
expressed his love of matter, evolution and 'the universal Christ'.
I recalled the first seven years of my own life as a Jesuit, studying
in the Ohio Valley, which coincided with Teilhard's years in New
York, and the fascination with his work even then, which was to
increase after he died, as his major works began to appear in
English. I can remember looking in a bookshop window in
Chicago where his *Letters from Hastings* were displayed. They had
been written to family and friends, from his west facing room at
Ore Place overlooking the Channel and Downs. In one of them he
mentioned the place where I live as a place with many schools.
Indeed I now live in the former grounds of a girls' secondary
school, founded in 1908, the year Teilhard began theology at
Hastings, and which like most of the private schools with which
Bexhill was then blessed, never recovered from the evacuation of
1939, when this coast – recalling the Conqueror's landing at nearby
Pevensey! – was a potential front line. In his talk at the Ore Place
dedication, the Chair of Hastings District Council, pointing towards the west, remarked that this was Teilhard's view when he
was here.

35. Pierre Teilhard de Chardin, *Hymn of the Universe* (NY: Harper & Row,
1961), p 87.

Teilhard's seminal and mystical vision still inspires. He is perhaps, as Ursula King remarked in Hastings Museum after a lecture there by geologist Ken Brooks on Teilhard's Sussex fossils
donated to the museum, 'more relevant now than ever'. Indeed in
his 'continental evolution' which he developed in China, he was a
precursor of today's 'Gaia hypothesis'. Of his scientific contribution, including specimens named after him in London Natural
History Museum, only paleontologists can judge. But for many
admirers in our 'planet in peril', his poetic, mystical vision relating evolution and human lives to the cosmic universal Christ is an
inspiration. Few modern thinkers have made such an impact.
Teilhard was, as we have noticed, ambiguous about 'progress' in
evolution and in the 'noosphere'. Yet his synthesis, grounded in
Saints Paul and John and the Greek fathers, and his demonstration of the compatibility of evolution with Christianity, remain
ahead of his own time and relevant in our own. Teilhard under-
stood biospheric connectedness, and he went further, connecting
'all things' and the whole universe to Jesus Christ.

With Newman, Teilhard, John Seymour, and millions of our
contemporaries, we anticipate in God's kingdom, final transformation and consummation. God's kingdom does not develop from
planetary evolution – if indeed evolution can be said to 'develop',
nor is it a 'project' that we can 'build'. God's kingdom is future
through and in Jesus Christ, the 'Omega Point', for which we can
prepare ourselves and our imperiled planet entrusted to us. It is to
Jesus Christ, of and within and ahead of our evolving biosphere,
to whom we now turn.

CHAPTER THREE

Jesus Lord of Climate and Evolution

Now Philip was from Bethsaida, the city of Andrew and Peter. Philip found Nathanael, and said to him, 'We have found him of whom Moses in the law and also the prophets wrote, Jesus of Nazareth, the son of Joseph.' Nathanael said to him, 'Can anything good come out of Nazareth?' Philip said to him, 'Come and see' (Jn 1:44-46).

The Scottish poet, Edwin Muir, said that in a visit to Italy he realised that God had walked the earth. 'Although the pagan gods had visited the earth and communed with men, they did not assume the burden of our flesh, live our life, and die our death, but after their intervention withdrew into impenetrable privacy.'[1] In Jesus of Nazareth, however, God entered our earth community in all its biodiversity. This evolving earth, with its fragile climate, wherein God lived our life, died our death, and arose and is present, is a varied community with myriad species and habitats. In a word first popularised in 1985 by W.G. Rosen, earth is 'biodiverse'. The Rio Earth Summit (1992) described biodiversity as 'the variety of living organisms from all sources including *inter alia*, terrestrial, marine, and other aquatic ecosystems and the ecological complexes of which they are a part: this includes diversity within species, between species and of ecosystems.'[2] All we have to do is walk in a local woodland, climb a hill, gaze into a garden pond, or nurture some soil to recognise how astonishingly biodiverse local ecosystems are. This is our earth in which Jesus lived among us. Now unfortunately we also notice our own species' detrimental impact, and even extinction, of life on earth. In Michigan, for ex-

---

1. Edwin Muir, *An Autobiography* (London: The Hogarth Press, 1956), p 278.
2. In Martin J. Hodson and Margot R. Hodson, *Cherishing the Earth, How to Care for God's Creation* (Oxford: Monarch, 2008), p 31.

ample, where I grew up, the native Americans tearfully signed away their traditional biodiverse forests and waters to white colonisers in 1836. By 1890, when the frontier, whose infinite resource illusion still pervades the American psyche, was declared closed, there remained few remnants of virgin forests, almost no white pine, and a much diminished biodiversity in the mitten shaped green, gold and blue peninsula that is Michigan.

As I write here in the UK, despite the sombre warnings and targets voiced at the Copenhagen climate summit, a debate still rages about present and future lifestyles. Some people, dwindling climate sceptics among them, hope to continue burning what fossil fuel remains, including abundant coal, while also building and expanding expensive, dangerous, and vulnerable nuclear plants, and to pursue 'economic growth' indefinitely. Others, who like the native Americans opt for quality, wish to 'live simply' that others may live, to conserve and insulate, and to reduce fossil fuel use while investing in research, development, deployment, and storage of sustainable alternative energies. As a nation Scotland continues to be a world leader, having set targets of an 80% reduction of emissions by 2050, and an admirable 42% by 2020 which include Scotland's air and ship emissions. On the outcome of this debate hinges the future of life on this planet.

As Christians, followers of God who in Jesus became flesh and inhabited the earth, we share with all faiths the challenge to cherish and restore our diminished biosphere, and to engage and integrate with the quality alternative movement. Moreover, we are challenged to offer our distinctive contribution as Christians, as incarnation and resurrection people, to demonstrate prophetically to fellow Christians, and to all faiths, as church leaders did admirably at Copenhagen, that we are involved and why. We owe it to our fragmented and ecologically confused society to interpret the Christ event while interpreting the reality of our planet being literally destroyed and burned by humanity; and to correlate these two interpretations. We can offer our contemporaries, in David Tracey's words, 'an interpretation of the Christ Event in dialectical correlation to the situation.'[3] In a conference on religious

3. David Tracey, *The Analogical Imagination; Christian Theology and the Culture of Pluralism* (NY: Crossroad, 1981), p 340.

education in Ireland, Dermot Lane observed, 'It is important, therefore, to have some sense of the socio-cultural context in which the message of Christianity is to be taught. Faith exists only as inculturated in particular historical, social and cultural forms.'[4]

Eyewitnesses of Jesus?
Often when we interpret – or reinterpret – the Jesus Christ event for these contexts, we begin with our creeds or with the first Christian writers, especially with the synoptic gospels and Paul as well as our own experience of Jesus Christ, but rarely with the fourth gospel. Here I suggest we broaden this procedure some-what by including John who, like Mark, begins at 'the beginning'. 'In the beginning was the Word, and the Word was with God, and the Word was God' (Jn 1:1). Debate about the final author of John continues – was he John the son of Zebedee, the beloved disciple, an anonymous genius, one, or two, final redactors …? Recently, and intriguingly, Richard Bauckham proposed that we revisit the fragmentary testimony of Papias, Bishop of Hierapolis around 130CE. Papias tried to meet and interview eye (and ear) witnesses who had experienced Jesus literally 'in the flesh', while Jesus lived and taught among us. Papias also made efforts to meet others who had known eyewitnesses. Geographically Papias was well posi-tioned to do so, for Hierapolis was at the meeting point of two busy roads, one running east to west, from Syrian Antioch to Ephesus, the other southeast to Attalia in Pamphylia and north-west to Smyrna. There Papias was able to investigate reports and traditions from near Jesus' own milieu, and from Palestinian Christians who settled in Hierapolis.[5] As a boy, Papias, a third generation Christian, met and questioned some he described as 'elder' eyewitnesses and 'elders' who had known eyewitnesses. Papias collected '*logia*' or sayings of Jesus in a five chapter booklet. Tantalisingly, these are lost, except for the famous prologue, pre-served by church historian Eusebius, and a few other fragments

---

4. Dermot Lane, *Challenges Facing Religious Education in Contemporary Ireland* (Dublin: Veritas, 2008), p 11.
5. Richard Bauckham, *Jesus and the Eyewitnesses, The Gospels as Eyewitness Testimony* (Cambridge: Eerdmanns, 2006), p 15.

preserved by Eusebius and by Irenaeus. The prologue, dedicated to an unknown person, is very interesting:

> I shall not hesitate to put into properly ordered form for you everything I learned carefully in the past from the elders and noted down well, for the truth of which I vouch. For unlike most people I did not enjoy those who have much to say but those who teach the truth. Nor did I enjoy those who recall someone else's commandments, but those who remember the commandments given by the Lord to the faith, and proceeding from the truth itself. And if by chance anyone who had been in attendance on the elders came my way I inquired about the words of the elders – what Andrew and Peter said, or Philip or Thomas or James, or John or Matthew or any other of the Lord's disciples, and whatever Aristion and the elder John the Lord's disciples were saying. For I did not think that information from books would profit me as much as information from a living and surviving voice.[6]

Papias, clearly, was a stickler for eyewitness testimony to Jesus' words and deeds. Those he considered reliable 'elders' were either eyewitnesses or had known eyewitnesses, two of whom, Aristion and the Elder John, lived well into Papias' lifetime. The latter, said Papias, was neither one of the twelve, nor John of Zebedee, but the beloved disciple and author of the fourth gospel, who had remained alive long after Jesus ascended (Jn 21:23-24). Papias' testimony is consistent with 1 John, 'That which was from the beginning, which we have seen with our eyes, which we have looked upon and touched with our hands, concerning the word of life – the life was made manifest, and we saw it, and testify to it, and proclaim to you, the eternal life which was with the Father and was made manifest to us – that which we have seen and heard we proclaim also to you' (1 Jn 1-3). Intriguingly the same writer twice refers to himself as 'the elder' (2 Jn 1:1; 3 Jn 1:1).

In his preface, therefore, Papias describes a time when the

---

6. Eusebius, *Church History*, 3.39. 3-4, in J. B. Lightfoot, J. P. Harmer, and M. W. Holmes, *The Apostolic Fathers* (Leicester: Appodos, 1990), p 314.

sons of Zebedee were dead, the synoptic gospel writers and John 'the Elder' still lived, and the latter was composing the fourth gospel. Bauckham writes:

> Of all the Asiatic elders it seems that he alone could be designated simply as 'the Elder' without ambiguity. This usage of Papias corresponds rather strikingly with the usage of the second and third Johannine letters, whose author designates himself simply as 'the Elder' (2 Jn 1; 3 Jn 1). This is a remarkable usage, because it is hard to find a parallel to the use, in the prescript of a letter where the author and recipient(s) are specified, of a title of this kind without a personal name ... If, as I believe, the same author was responsible for the gospel of John and all three Johannine letters, then our argument leads to the conclusion that John the Elder was the Beloved Disciple and the author of the gospel of John.[7]

In interpreting Jesus' life on earth we often begin with the infancy stories of Matthew and Luke, or perhaps with the oldest of our four gospels, Mark's 'the beginning of the good news', echoing Genesis and leading into the wilderness with the Baptist and the wild animals. In the light of Papias' preface, however, we may also find what Ignatius Loyola called 'fruit' by noting John's own prologue which begins significantly with 'In the beginning ...', and by including Jesus' ecological metaphors and actions narrated in John's gospel.

John's prologue was composed two millennia before primordial fireball and evolution theories.[8] Yet the prologue provides an apt 'beginning' for dialogue with empirical science about origins and evolution. God's care, presence, compassion and love for God's evolving biosphere is 'from the beginning' until now and forever. Every instant is creation, every being that evolves, with all its symbiotic fellow creatures is ultimately dependent on God's sustaining love. All and each creature are frailer than an

7. Bauckham, *Jesus and the Eyewitnesses*, pp 421-423.
8. Leo Donovan SJ, 'Evolution', in *The New Dictionary of Theology*, Joseph A. Komanchak, Mary Collins, and Dermot A. Lane, eds (Dublin: Gill & Macmillan, 1987), pp 363-387.

autumn leaf. To attest our contingency means no matter how fit or adaptive we are, if God lets go, even evolution's selected survivors cease. But thankfully – and hopefully – God never does. John's prologue does not sidestep our broken condition, rather he implies it (Jn 1:11-12). Our inherent frailty, pictured in Genesis, coheres well with what we know about the evolving biosphere. The human species is morally fickle and prone to greed from birth. Adam, from *adamah*, is related to all other soil beings. And yet, as God's image, we are responsible for mediating God's own supportive love for his creation. This is the earth community, including sinful yet responsible humans, into which God's Word in Jesus, empties himself. In Jesus, God is incarnate in our cosmos, the seed and source of future transformation of creation. In Karl Rahner's words, in Jesus is 'the embryonically final beginning of the glorification and divinisation of the whole of reality.'[9]

John's testimony, like that of Paul, includes his experience of Jesus risen. Unlike Paul, John's experience also reaches back into Jesus' itinerant ministry. We do not know whether John was from Nazareth or elsewhere in Galilee or Judea. But, as the beloved disciple, he was familiar with Jesus' appreciation of the earth community. Through John's description of Jesus when meeting Nathanael as 'of Nazareth, son of Joseph', we note, as do the synoptics, that Jesus was a village craftsman of Nazareth, almost certainly supplementing family income by growing food in family fields on the chalk and marl ridge (Jn 1:45-49). Hence Jesus' familiarity with the shade of fig trees. John often associates Jesus with water, in Cana, at the lake, with the Baptist, at Jacob's well, in the washing of his disciple's feet, and with the water from his open side, and again, as risen, at the lake. 'Christ is never without water', ('*numquam sine aqua Christus*'), said the African Tertullian, echoing John's gospel.

John's Jesus was familiar with fields ripe for harvest, with autumn and spring sowing, with harvesting itself, and with shepherds and sheep. He compares himself to a good shepherd. At an outdoor meal Jesus relates bread to his flesh. In a famous Johannine

---

9. Karl Rahner, 'Dogmatic Questions on Easter', *Theological Investigations*, Vol 4 (NY: Seabury, 1946), p 126.

discourse he also compares himself to a vine, his disciples to branches, his Father to the vinedresser. Prunings from vines were not wasted, but were collected and burned, their ashes returned to the soil. In visits to Jerusalem, Jesus often visited the peaceful plantation of Gethsemane on the Mount. 'Judas, who betrayed him, also knew the place; for Jesus often met there with his disciples' (Jn 18:2). John's passion account includes the last meal, the foot washing, the walk across the valley to the olive garden, the open side and the 'woman' at the cross, death and burial in 'a garden' and again with garden and gardener connotations evoking the older Genesis story and new creation, the appearance to another woman, from Magdala, where he is mistaken for the gardener (Gen 2:15; Jn 20:17-18). John also describes a final appearance at the lake (water again), some fish, and breakfast, another 'last meal' together. His final words to Peter compare Peter to a shepherd, commissioned to feed Christ's, the Good Shepherd's lambs and sheep (Jn 21:9-17).

Infancy and Childhood
We owe the familiar infancy stories which enhance Christmas to Matthew and Luke. They were compiled later than were the resurrection traditions, and the traditions of Jesus' words and deeds after he left Nazareth.[10] The infancy narratives, therefore, were not redacted by eyewitnesses. Nevertheless, both Matthew and Luke – and Luke is by far the longer account – abound with implications about 'Jesus and the earth' to quote the title of Bishop James Jones widely read book.[11] Like John's gospel, both infancy accounts relate Jesus to Nazareth. Matthew does so in a way that evokes the peaceable kingdom, relating Jesus to Davidic kingship, and what we may call eschatological ecology. 'He went and dwelt in a city called Nazareth, that what was spoken by the prophets might be fulfilled, "He shall be called a Nazarene" (Mt 2:23).' Matthew here cleverly puns on the *nazir*, or root of Jesse from whom would come the awaited ruler who would bring harmony among humans and other sensate creatures (Is 11:1-9).

---

10. Raymond E. Brown, *The Birth of the Messiah* (London: Geoffrey Chapman, 1993), pp 26-29.
11. James Jones, *Jesus and the Earth* (London: SPCK, 2007).

Among other Matthean ecological hints are the royal connotations of Bethlehem itself, shared with Luke's account, and the
star. The wise magus Balaam who foretold the star is popular in
early Christian iconography including his association with a wise
and articulate donkey (Num 22:21-35). In Matthew three 'magi'
offer the child elements of the earth as gifts. In our churches and
crèches Luke's shepherds and sheep join Matthew's magi become
kings! There is sensitivity in imaginatively blending the two accounts as we do, for Christ comes to all of us, kings and shepherds,
town and country people. We see this universality of the incarnation in the Christmas worship of city families, of country people
in village churches, and of the royal family at Sandringham.
Joseph's dream guiding the holy family to Egypt echoes the
dreams of his ancestor and namesake, the patriarch Joseph, who
was familiar with food insecurity and with abundance, as now are
we (Gen 47:1-26).

Luke's infancy, as we notice with the shepherds and sheep and
manger, is pervaded with ecological connotations. According to
the late Lukan scholar George Caird, the annunciation and birth
are about new creation. 'What Luke is here concerned to tell us is
that Jesus entered on the status of sonship at his birth by a new cre-
ative act of that same Holy Spirit which at the beginning had
brooded over the waters of chaos. It is the new creation that is the
real miracle of Jesus' birth and the real theme of Gabriel's annunciation and Mary's wondering awe.'[12] There is no historical record
of the census described by Luke, but Luke's account does remind
us of Joseph's Davidic descent, and explains Jesus' birth in a
Judean town – the royal motif, as in Matthew's star and magi. To
Luke we owe the story of the swaddling clothes and manger,
which in the Jewish scriptures as in our crèches, is forever associated with the domestic ox and ass, and has enriched homes,
churches, shops, and market squares for centuries, and still at-
tracts children. The child is, after all, 'fully human', inter-related,
as are we, to all earth creatures, and as 'true God' is reconciler of
all creation, including kings, shepherds and animals, all of whom
are represented in our crèches. After a ceremony in the Jerusalem

12. George Caird, *Saint Luke* (Harmondsworth: Penguin, 1985), p 53.

temple, Luke's holy family returned to Nazareth, 'their own city', about which Nathanael of neighbouring Cana was so dismissive, where Jesus grew in age, wisdom, and stature.

Nazareth

The gospels say little explicitly, although much is implied, about Jesus' Nazareth years, the longest part of his life, during which he learned, especially from older men of the village about the soil. We may contemplate Jesus there, from the agrarian perspective of the Jewish scriptures.[13] The Jews considered themselves a covenanted people, which included the land. 'I will remember my covenant with Jacob, and I will remember my covenant with Isaac and my covenant with Abraham, and I will remember the land' (Lev 26:42). Urban biblical scholars and preaching ministers in our churches often overlook Jesus' relationships and interdependence to patrimonial extended family fields, the *agrous* from which many of his teaching metaphors were drawn. Ellen Davis observes:

> Agrarianism is a way of thinking and ordering life in community that is based on the health of the land and of living creatures. Often out of step with the prevailing values of wealth, technology, and political and military domination, the mindset and practices that constitute agrarianism have been marginalised by the powerful within most 'history-making' cultures across time, including that of ancient Israel. Yet, agrarianism is the way of thinking predominant among the biblical writers, who very often do not represent the interests of the powerful.[14]

The valleys in lower Galilee run east to west, and are fertile and well watered, a land 'of milk and honey'. These were soon appropriated by elites, Herodians and Romans in the time of Jesus, hence his parables' inclusion of tenants, workers, and dispossessed.

---

13. Edward P. Echlin, *The Cosmic Circle, Jesus and Ecology* (Dublin: Columba Press, 2004), p 63.
14. Ellen F. Davis, *Scripture, Culture, and Agriculture, An Agrarian Reading of the Bible* (NY: CUP, 2007), p 1.

Peasant families lived and farmed, in partial self sufficiency, on the thinner soiled ridges. The Nazareth ridge was especially fertile, and irrigated by a spring and wadi. There is still evidence of iron age terracing, towers, and presses. Crops known to Jesus included cereals, brassicas, root and forage crops, olives, grapes, pomegranates, dates, and possibly some apples. Preserving for the winter rainy season included drying fruit in the burning summer sun, and deep storage similar to our carbon neutral 'clamping'. Every family field, like a modern garden or allotment, has its own characteristics. 'There's an undying difference in the corner of a field', said Monaghan farmer and poet Patrick Kavanagh. A farmer or grower becomes familiar with every rock, den, bush, slope, ridge, sun spot, and soil texture. Fields are relatively green and gold in growing season, multi-hued and white at harvest. A food grower is always preparing for the late winter 'hunger gap'. This explains the increasing relevance for partly self sufficient people, which many of us now are, of the petition, 'Give us this day our daily bread', or 'bread for tomorrow'.[15]

Through his education by parents and elders, by synagogue readings and by the teaching of the soil itself, Jesus learned about God's creation and his special place within it.[16] We noticed John's hint of village rivalry in Nathanael's question to Philip of Bethsaida, 'Can anything good come out of Nazareth?' (Jn 1:44-6). In fact Nazareth was relatively well endowed on the southern edge of Galilee, of around 2,000 people and 30,000 square metres. Families lived in small houses around shared courtyards. The more northern ridges were less suitable for plants and stock than were Nazareth and the valleys. In addition to water from springs and wadis, the people also harvested winter rain, storing it in cisterns for the long burning dry season.

We are learning today that even into advanced maturity, and indeed old age, a person's childhood pervasively influences his adult perceptions and actions. This was no less true of the human

---

15. Jonathan Ross, *Archaeology and the Galilean Jesus* (Trinity: Harrisburg, 2000), p 67.
16. John Meier, *A Marginal Jew, Rethinking the Historical Jesus*, Vol I (NY: Doubleday, 1991), pp 273, 278.

Jesus and his memorable teaching and deeds. Joseph and Jesus were *tectons*, craftsmen (Mk 6:3; Mt 13:55). In a relatively large family they would have supplemented a craftsman's income by food growing and stock rearing in family *agrous*. Villages and their adjacent fields, or hinterland, and small spaces within villages, formed an economic partly self sufficient entity. Villages produced just enough food (in good weather). Hence the fundamental importance Jesus later gave to a young man's *agrous*, as a precious inheritance he would leave, or transmit to another family member, to follow Jesus (Mk 10:29; Mt 19-29). Villages had to produce most of what they consumed, plus extortionate taxes in kind for Roman and Herodian occupiers. Hence the later resentment of Jesus' association with tax collectors.

As a young adult, Jesus left his Nazareth family and home, and joined for a time the community of John the wilderness baptiser. The evangelist John locates the Baptist in the Jordan valley, and in Perea, which was probably John's last base because, according to Josephus, John was imprisoned and executed at Macherus, a fortress east of the Dead Sea (Jn 3:23-26). Jesus was baptised by John and later baptised others. While in John's wilderness community, Jesus deepened his conviction that he was sent by God to preach the nearness of the kingdom, already beginning in his own life, words and actions.[17] The Baptist recognised Jesus' mission, and preached him as sent from God. 'You yourselves bear me witness, that I said, I am not the Christ, but I have been sent before him. He who has the bride is the bridegroom; the friend of the bridegroom, who stands and hears him, rejoices greatly at the bridegroom's voice; therefore this joy of mine is now full. He must increase, but I must decrease' (Jn 3:28-30). We can notice Jesus' affinity with the natural world, henceforth including wilderness places, which remained with him to the end. The gospels say that, while in the wilderness, Jesus was tempted by Satan, but that he remained steadfast in his Nazareth and wilderness conviction that he had a special mission in 'his Father's kingdom'. Jesus left John's wilderness lifestyle and the wilderness itself to live for the remainder of his life an alternative itinerant lifestyle, not with

---

17. Seán Freyne, *Jesus a Jewish Galilean* (London: Continuum, 2004), p 41.

John's wilderness asceticism, but as a prophetic alternative to the relative security of life within a settled kinship group.

Itinerant Ministry

On leaving the wilderness, Jesus chose as a base not Nazareth 'where he had been brought up', but the fishing port Capernaum, in 'the valley' on the gleaming inland lake. We noticed that when Jesus' family returned from Egypt to Nazareth, Matthew invoked the 'nazir' or shoot metaphor associated with the peaceable kingdom (Mt 2:23; Is 11:1). Now, when Jesus chose Capernaum as 'his own city', Matthew associates Jesus with another inclusive Jewish text, this time evoking water and fertility. 'He went and dwelt in Capernaum by the sea, in the territory of Zebulun and Naphtali, that what was spoken by the prophet Isaiah might be fulfilled: "The land of Zebulun and the land of Naphtali, toward the sea, across the Jordan, Galilee of the Gentiles"' (Mt 4:13-15; Is 9:1-2). These texts are evocative for our time of climate disturbance and the concomitant suffering of creation. Jesus, when we contemplate the Jewish and Christian scriptures imaginatively, is the inclusive Lord of climate, soil, water and earth peace. Capernaum, like the Nazareth ridge, is a fertile, biodiverse ecosystem, including the lake with its aquatic community and fertile basaltic soil in the hinterland. Then, as now, the fertile fields and hills were rich with cereals and fruit. Capernaum deepened Jesus' experience of the natural world, which now included the biodiverse lake with its birds, fish, and animals, and the west winds over Migdal, also called Tarichaeae, a reference to salt. Although Peter and Andrew, James, John and Philip and other principal disciples were from the lake region or 'valley', and the fish became an early Christian symbol, most of Jesus' memorable metaphors derive from the hill country where he lived the formative years of his life. Yet there were also lake symbols: his apostles were to be 'fishers of men', and there was the storm at sea and swelling nets, and final meal, and commissioning of Peter on the shore. Also significant for our time of melting glaciers there was Mount Hermon's snow and aquifers which fed the Jordan and the lake. At Capernaum Jesus experienced the truth of the scriptures that 'dew from Hermon waters the mountains of Zion.'[18] Although based in Capernaum, possibly in Peter's house, Jesus travelled through Palestine, preaching, teaching, and healing and exorcising, in country, villages, and wilderness. Eric Eve observes that 'his healing and exorcising activity formed an important part of his ministry, vital if not central to his role, as a symbolic demonstration of the coming of God's rule.'[19]

In his itinerant and inclusive lifestyle, Jesus was in the tradition of Abraham, ancestor of many nations (Gen 17:5-7). Jesus prayed to God as Father and Lord. In Jesus' words, 'I thank thee Father, Lord of heaven and earth' (Mt 11:25; cf Is 40:12; 42:5; 48:13). In patriarchal societies, a father, usually assisted by sons, was the principal provider of life's necessities. To thank God as Lord was to acknowledge God as creator of all that is. Jesus lived within the Sabbath and Jubilee culture of trust in God, Father and Lord, for life's necessities, 'Foxes have holes, and birds of the air have nests; but the Son of man has nowhere to lay his head' (Mt 8:20; Lk 9:58). God did indeed provide for Jesus and his followers especially through reasonably stable climate and the gifts of creation dependent on climate. God's providence, for Jesus and his disciples and for ourselves, is principally mediated through the land and the care and sharing of our fellow human creatures. Jesus' trust in his Father's provision for himself and his followers, mediated through the land and people, is reflected in Luke's account of Jesus' commission of seventy two missionary disciples:

> I send you out as lambs in the midst of wolves. Carry no purse, no bag, no sandals; and salute no one on the road. Whatever house you enter, first say, 'Peace be to this house!' And if a son of peace is there, your peace shall rest upon him; but if not, it shall return to you. And remain in the same house, eating and drinking what they provide, for the labourer deserves his wages; do not go from house to house (Lk 10:3-7).

This Sabbath and Jubilee ethos is an ideal which, if widely and

---

18. Freyne, *Jesus a Jewish Galilean*, pp 48-53.
19. Eric Eve, *The Healer from Nazareth, Jesus' Miracles in Historical Context* (London: SPCK, 2009), p 165.

literally followed, would be impractical for a self sufficient economy based on shared kinship holdings. But it is an ideal which
teaches much about God's kingdom, and was lived by Jesus as an
effective sign of that kingdom.[20]

Within this radically prophetic alternative lifestyle, dependent on God's providence and human sharing fellowship, Jesus
preached the dawning of God's kingdom, using metaphors
drawn from peasant and lake life. We are especially familiar with
parables of seeds, the good shepherd, the good Samaritan, the lost
sheep, the mustard bush, the vineyard, the net bursting with fish,
and many more. Jesus preached and taught in more than words.
He was in the inclusive tradition of his remote ancestors,
Abraham and Sarah, welcoming people who found God in diverse ways. This is important for his followers today when different 'faiths' unite and work together to stabilise climate, care for
earth's creatures, and seek an economy of quality, not infinite
'growth'.[21] He also preached – and illustrated – the coming kingdom in his prophetic actions, notably in shared meals, some of
which were outside (Mt 15:32-38; Jn 6:1-14). These meals, inclusive of the fertility of the local soil community, and open to people
'from East and West', were enacted parables of the inclusive kingdom. New Testament scholar Bruce Chilton observes,

> The paradigmatic link between the kingdom and fellowship at
> meals is widely accepted as an established feature of what
> Jesus taught, and with ample warrant. Meals in Jesus' fellow-
> ship became practical parables where meaning was as evoc-
> ative as his verbal parables which have consumed much more
> scholarly interest. To join in his meals was, in effect, to antici-
> pate the kingdom, in a certain manner, the manner delineated
> by Jesus.[22]

Jesus' association with water continued throughout his life, as

---

20. Freyne, *Jesus a Jewish Galilean*, p 118.
21. Gerald O'Collins SJ, *Salvation for All God's Other People* (Oxford: OUP,
2008), esp pp 12-16, 55-56.
22. Bruce Chilton, *Eucharistic Theologies from Jesus through Johannine Circles*
(NY: E. J. Brill, 1994), pp 126-131.

did his affinity with territorial wilderness and thinly populated country. He frequently withdrew to 'lonely places' to think and pray and to teach his closest disciples. Yet, as we noticed, his asceticism – or, in today's parlance, 'living lightly' – differed from that of the wilderness Baptist. Indeed Jesus was accused of enjoying 'eating and drinking', and of mingling with despised tax collectors and 'sinners'. Jesus responded, 'I have come not to call the righteous but sinners to repentance' (Lk 5:32).

Soon after leaving John's community, Jesus made a return visit to Nazareth 'where he had been brought up'. In his well known account of Jesus' return, Luke says he went to the synagogue on the Sabbath and, 'as was his custom', stood up to read from the scriptures. His text was from the later Isaiah's words about the expected future prophet and jubilee (Is 61:1-2; cf 58:6). When he commented that this text was fulfilled in himself and his ministry, his former neighbours praised him as Joseph's son. They were annoyed, however, when he said famously that a prophet is not appreciated in his own country, giving two examples from Elijah and Elisha that illustrate his own universalism. He recalled the drought when Elijah ministered to a Zarepeth widow in the coastal area. The widow, though starving and with a dying son, gave the prophet some precious bread, water, and oil. Elijah then resuscitated her son (1 Kgs 17:8-24). Jesus then recalled how Elisha, when leprosy was widespread, visited Naaman, a Syrian leper, and told him to wash in the Jordan, and his leprosy was cleansed (2 Kgs 5:1-8). This recognition of the two prophets for healing outsiders so enraged Jesus' former neighbours that they expelled him from his home town on the ridge (Lk 4:14-30).

Jesus addressed recurrent food anxiety, both in his trusting itinerant lifestyle and in his teaching. Food (and water) anxiety recurs intermittently in self-sufficient peasant societies and, increasingly, in globalised consumer societies, as we are noticing. He taught his followers to pray that God's will be done on earth as in heaven, and to petition the Father for daily bread, or the foundational necessities of life. According to Matthew and Luke, Jesus illustrated his teaching with the trusting birds of the air and the carefree wildflowers. He noted the absence of food anxiety in the birds, yet God feeds them. Similarly, the carefree flowers of the meadow neither toil nor spin, yet are more beautiful than Solomon in his glory. Then, in words that have puzzled some, Jesus uses an *a fortiori* comparison: if God cares for these creatures, even more does he provide for people. His *a fortiori* comparing ravens, wildflowers, and people actually teaches the value of all to God.

Flora and fauna, vegetable and sensate life, the whole earth biosphere and its biodiversity are precious. Jesus' use of *a fortiori* shows that his teaching is not sentimental romanticism – people are special, for we alone are God's image, responsible, under God, for earth's welfare. Jesus' teaching about life's necessities, food and clothing, urges hope in God's universal providence and kingdom. 'Your heavenly Father knows that you need them all. But seek first his kingdom and his righteousness, and all these things shall be yours as well' (Mt 6:32-33). Jesus' teaching includes active hope. He says that we need not be anxious about the future, tomorrow, because the time to secure tomorrow's necessities is tomorrow; but he adds that we also need to work today, 'sufficient for today is its own trouble' (Mt 6:25-34; Lk 12:22-30).

These words about today, in a context of food, clothing, and shelter, show that our trust and hope cannot be a passive romanticism. Life's necessities do not fall like gentle rain, we also work 'for a living' or in what we can describe as 'partial self sufficiency', which is never easy, hence today's 'own troubles'. Like ourselves, the apostle Paul grasped the importance of active hope: his was a travelling lifestyle, dependent on Jesus' disciples for food and shelter, yet he also ministered by teaching and, at times, by working as a tradesman. We cannot hope for God to stabilise the climate, securing our food and shelter, unless we ourselves live in active hope, urgently contributing to climate change mitigation, and by adapting and helping others to adapt to ineluctable human induced 'climate chaos'.

Beyond Galilee
Jesus, in his itinerant ministry, like Elijah and Elisha, travelled beyond Galilee and Judea to coastal and northern gentile territories.

He showed sympathy for pet dogs in his meeting with a woman from Tyre. When she requested that he heal her daughter, he replied that he was sent to the children of Israel and could not throw children's bread to small dogs. Her reply that even small dogs eat crumbs under their master's table so moved him that he replied, 'Woman great is your faith. Be it done as you requested' (Mt 15:21-28). Kenneth Bailey comments, 'A new paradigm of who God is and to whom he extends his love (through Jesus) will inevitably struggle to be born as a result of this dramatic scene. In the process the woman's faith is rendered unforgettable and is, like the faith of the woman who anointed Jesus in the house of Simon the leper (Mk 14:3-9), proclaimed wherever the gospel is preached.'[23]

As his ministry approached its climax, and Jerusalem beckoned, Jesus journeyed with close disciples northwards to the 'region of Caesarea Philippi', at Mount Hermon and the apparent source of the Jordan. The mountain is an impressive 8000 feet at its summit, and was venerated as the source of the (then) pure river and Lake Galilee (or Gennesareth). Both Jews and gentiles appreciated the mountain's gift of water, the *sine qua non* nurturer of life, especially apparent in middle east dry seasons. There was a shrine to Pan, vegetation deity of fertility and panpipes, wine, music and dancing, closely associated with the Greek god Dionysius. Hence the name Baneas for the region. Jews venerated Hermon along with Mount Tabor in the south. 'You created the north and the south. Hermon and Tabor rejoice at your name' (Ps 89:12). Caesar Augustus had given the district, with its shrine in the red rock cliff, to Herod the Great who erected a temple there to Caesar. Herod Philip named his settlement there after Caesar. It became a Jewish outpost, then later a Byzantine centre called Baneas, a wilderness, a Russian tourist site, a French mandate, a Syrian village, and since 1967 a controversial Israeli outpost. In those fertile environs Jesus continued to structure his community. Mark and Matthew say he named Simon Peter, or 'rock', in that time and place. In Matthew's famous and sometimes controversial words,

23. Kenneth E. Bailey, *Jesus Through Middle Eastern Eyes, Cultural Studies in the Gospels* (London: SPCK, 2009), pp 224-225.

'You are Peter, and on this rock I will build my church' (Mt 16:18;
Mk 8:27-30; cf Jn 1:40-42). John's gospel adds that the risen Jesus
commissioned Peter at another fertile setting, the shore of the
gleaming biodiverse lake (Jn 21:15-17). Today, as glaciers melt
and the Jordan dwindles, the lake falls, and climate change deepens, we may ask ourselves if Christ's followers should contemplate these ecological connotations for church leadership.[24]

Jerusalem

After the visit to the Caesarea Philippi region Jesus began his final
journey, preaching God's kingdom. He realised that he had an important role in the kingdom's growth on earth, and that he would
be rejected by the Jewish and Roman establishment. The late C. F.
D. Moule is doubtless correct that Jesus did not make the
Jerusalem journey deliberately to die, but he did realise it might
cost him his life, especially after his symbolic act in the temple and
his attracting of followers.[25] The accounts of his final entry note
that he rode into Jerusalem on a borrowed donkey, enacting the
prophecy of Zechariah. 'Your king comes to you; triumphant and
victorious is he, humble and riding on an ass, on a colt the foal of
an ass' (Zech 9:9). Zechariah also refers to living water, 'On that
day living waters shall flow out from Jerusalem, half of them to
the eastern sea and half of them to the western sea; it shall continue
in summer as in winter' (Zech 14:8). People recognised the donkey
symbolism by spreading palms and garments before Christ, the
awaited king on a donkey. According to the synoptics, it was at
this time that Jesus cleansed the temple of commerce, acting with
widely – and fatefully –noted authority.

There were also expectations of abundant fruit in God's awaited
kingdom (Rev 22:2). A story about Jesus and a barren fig tree has
puzzled many. Mark says that Jesus cursed a fruitless tree, and
that the following day his disciples found it withered (Mk 11:12-
22). Matthew reports the tree withered immediately (Mt 21:18-19).
When this legend is taken literally it disturbs people even today. I

---

24. Edward P. Echlin, 'Climate Change Theology', *New Blackfriars* (Autumn
2008), pp 71-79.
25. C. F. D. Moule, *The Origin of Christology* (Cambridge: CUP, 1977), p 109.

have been asked about it often. The story is just that, a symbolic story, which should not be taken as literal history. Marcan scholar Denis Nineham observes that it may have begun as a legend 'that grew in the telling'. For Jesus may have remarked that a tree near Jerusalem was not fruiting despite the dawning kingdom – and a legend grew that he had cursed the tree which then withered. Another possibility is that there was a dead fig on the way into Jerusalem and that a story arose that Jesus had cursed it.[26] Luke's accounts about Jesus and figs are more characteristic, as in Jesus' parable about an unproductive fig tree whose impatient owner wanted it uprooted, but whose gardener interceded for the tree, asking for another year to manure it. Jesus also noted that young leaves of figs are a sign of summer, harbingers of the kingdom. 'Look at the fig tree, and all the trees; as soon as they come out in leaf, you see for yourselves and know that the summer is already near' (Lk 21:29-30). Significantly, Jesus' ministry concluded in a favourite olive orchard.

After a farewell meal at Bethany, the home of Mary, Martha and Lazarus, Jesus asked his disciples to arrange a final meal in Jerusalem, at Passover, since known as the Last Supper. Jesus associated the bread and wine with his body and blood, and asked that the meal be repeated in his memory until he returned. With his closest disciples Jesus then retired to Gethsemane for the last time. Gethsemane was a favourite 'lonely place' during visits to Jerusalem. Luke says, 'Every day he was teaching in the temple, but at night he went out and lodged on the mount called Olivet' (Lk 21:37). Before tensions and my own flight emissions became intolerable, I visited Gethsemane several times, and was moved by the biodiversity and the sheep grazing peacefully there with birds resting on their back. I am told this is not unusual, but have seen it nowhere else.

Passion and Death
Jesus persisted in trust in God, his Father and Lord, during his arrest, trials, and death. New Testament scholar Seán Freyne

---

26. Denis Nineham, *Saint Mark, Pelikan Commentary* (Harmondsworth: Penguin, 1976), p 299.

notes that he shared the apocalyptic imagination of his Jewish
contemporaries whereby God's kingdom includes all creation:

> His was a faith that was grounded in a trust in the goodness of
> the creation as he had experienced it and reflected on its mys-
> terious but hidden processes. It was also a faith that had been
> nourished by the apocalyptic imagination that this creator
> God was still in charge of his world and had the power to make
> all things new again.[27]

There are intimations of sacred, earth inclusive kingship in
Jesus' trial and death, as there are in his birth and his life's teaching and actions (Jn 18:33-40; 19:3-22). Jesus was condemned to the
most heinous of deaths because he was perceived as a threat to
Herodians and imperial elites. It is evocative, especially for our
time of food insecurity, that Simon of Cyrene coming 'from the
fields' carried Jesus' cross, walking, says Luke, after him. Like
Jesus, Simon had cultivated food in 'the fields' of Palestine. He
was the first to carry the cross after Jesus (Lk 23:26). In describing
Jesus' death, John symbolises new creation, saying that when a
soldier opened Jesus' side with a lance, blood and water flowed
into the skull-shaped hill (Jn 19:34). As we noticed, Jesus refers to
Mary, his mother, as 'woman' and to the beloved disciple as her
son (Jn 19:25). John adds, 'in the place where he was crucified
there was a garden' (Jn 19:41).

The synoptics enrich their passion accounts with apocalyptic
symbolism: darkness, a cosmic quake, the temple curtain torn,
dead rising, all signifying new Israel, new creation, cosmic reconciliation. The quake and darkness may suggest cosmic compassion, as in the tenth century 'Dream of the Rood', 'Clouds of darkness swept across his shining splendour. All creation wept'; and
in the haunting Afro-American spiritual 'Were you there when
the sun refused to shine?' Jesus was buried in the garden, in a new
tomb, by faithful disciples – including Nicodemus and Joseph of
Arimathea. Wrapped in linen, Jesus was anointed with myrrh of
the balsam family which grows in Arabia and Somaliland, and
with aloes of the mideast lily family. The life, suffering, death,

---

27. Freyne, *Jesus a Jewish Galilean*, p 149.

burial, and resurrection of Jesus, Lord of climate and evolution, was and remains at the very centre of the earth.

The crucifixion when, as we noted, Jesus' blood flowed onto the earth, was inevitably a stumbling block to some of Jesus' followers. Even the apostle Thomas at first doubted the eyewitness testimony of those who had experienced Jesus risen.[28] Those who believed, then and now, recognise in Jesus risen the inauguration of God's kingdom and new creation. Jesus in his humanity, inter-related, as are we, with *adamah*, the whole soil community, is the New Adam, still in solidarity with the soil. Richard Bauckham writes:

> The Christian tradition at its most authentic has realised that the promise of God made in the bodily resurrection of Christ is holistic and all-encompassing: for whole persons, body and soul, for all the networks of relationship in human society that are integral to being human, and for the rest of creation also, from which humans in their bodiliness are not to be detached. In other words, it is God's creative renewal of his whole creation.[29]

In Mark's appendix Jesus appears to the eleven at table and tells them to preach the good news to all 'creation' (*ktsis*) (Mk 16:15). Exegetes remain hesitant about how universally 'creation' is to be interpreted. St Francis Assisi did, famously, preach even to the birds of Umbria. Within the deep tradition, enlightened by reception history, we can imaginatively include other creatures in the good news about our shared future in the kingdom. Luke imaginatively relates Jesus to the first Adam when, in Luke's Emmaus narrative, Cleopas and his companion recognise Jesus risen in the stranger they meet on the road who explains to them the scriptures. When he breaks bread with them, 'their eyes were opened; and they recognised him', echoing and reversing what Genesis says about Adam and Eve after they ate the forbidden

---

28. David J. Norman OFM, 'Doubt of the Resurrection of Jesus', *Theological Studies* (December 2008), pp 783-815.

29. Richard Bauckham, 'The Future of Jesus Christ', in Markus Bockmuehl, ed, *The Cambridge Companion to Jesus* (Cambridge: CUP, 2001), p 268.

fruit, 'their eyes were opened, and they knew that they were naked' (Lk 24:31; Gen 3:7).

In Christ the New Adam, God reconciles 'all things' in heaven and on earth, 'in him all the fullness of God was pleased to dwell, and through him to reconcile to himself all things, whether on earth or in heaven, making peace by the blood of his cross' (Col 1:19-20; cf Eph 1:9-10). St John, an eyewitness of the Christ event, testifies to the objective truth of the resurrection, 'He who saw it has borne witness – his testimony is true, and he knows that he tells the truth – that you also may believe' (Jn 19:35).

We cannot presume that God will intervene to unite us and the earth to Christ in the kingdom while we continue to disrupt the climate and destroy the earth. But we may hope that people everywhere will re-enter creation, and heal the earth in prophetic alternative lifestyles. Then, the restoration of 'all things', including a reconciled climate, will be completed at the *parousia*, when Jesus returns. Meanwhile, all creation groans and awaits what Paul intriguingly calls 'the revelation' of the children of God, when all creation will be liberated from its own suffering and enjoy the freedom of God's human children (Rom 8:19-23). That 'revelation' reminds us that we await in active hope (Mt 6:34). The risen Christ will return welcoming all creation into his kingdom, because we who are God's children, his sacral royal representatives, here and now and tomorrow, actively prepare for his coming. We must abandon the misconceptions that we are presumptuous or 'semi-Pelagian' when we actively hope by preparing for God's kingdom. As Benedict Viviano says, 'He will not force it on an unwilling and unready people. Our task in the time between is to remove obstacles to prepare the world for the kingdom'.[30] We must live justly and sustainably, stabilising the climate, letting biodiversity and fertility and glaciers regenerate, healing earth's suffering until we can confidently say '*maranatha*', 'Come Lord Jesus'. God's kingdom is indeed God's work, God's coming,

30. Benedict Viviano OP, *The Kingdom of God in History* (Wilmington: Michael Glazier, 1988), p 22; cf Hilary Marlow, *The Earth is the Lord's, A Biblical Response to Environmental Issues* (Cambridge: Grove Books Ltd, 2008), pp 25-26.

God's future. But we have a preparatory part, by living sustainably locally, in Christian ecology, as a living gospel, so that in the
flowering of the kingdom, 'at the name of Jesus every knee should
bow, in heaven and on earth and under the earth, and every
tongue confess that Jesus Christ is Lord, to the glory of God the
Father' (Phil 2:10-11; Rev 5:13).

CHAPTER FOUR

Towards a Prophetic Alternative

If we do not change our direction, we are likely to end up where we are headed.
Chinese Proverb

The shortest way home is to go all the way around the world.
G. K. Chesterton

Pictures from space of our fragile planet, vulnerable and alone, and the profound exclamations of astronauts, move us to wonder, and to appreciate our home. Sigmund Jahn says that he always knew earth was frail and vulnerable. 'But only when I saw it from space did I realise that our most urgent task is to cherish and preserve it.' For Edgar Mitchell, 'to glimpse our planet was to view the mystery of God'. The Chinese American astronaut, Taylor Wang, was reminded of a poignant Chinese story about a vulnerable, beautiful and endangered young girl, and becoming her admiring protector. 'That's how I felt seeing the earth for the first time – I could not help but love and cherish it.' Pondering the astronauts' reflections, I was struck by the similarity to Pierre Teilhard de Chardin's reminiscences about the Sussex countryside, especially in the frail evening light. After an interval of forty years, Teilhard recalled:

> The extraordinary solidity and intensity I found then in the English countryside, particularly at sunset when the Sussex woods were charged with all that 'fossil' life I was then hunting for from cliff to quarry in the wealden clay. There were moments indeed when it seemed to me that a sort of universal being was about to take shape suddenly in Nature before my very eyes.[1]

---

1. Pierre Teilhard de Chardin, *The Heart of Matter* (London: Collins, 1978), p 25.

We need inspiration from scientists and astronauts – and from mystics and poets like John Muir and Père Teilhard. We need global – and local – co-operation if we are to stabilise climate and preserve our planet, by cherishing and 'letting be' the varied biosystems of earth, from insects to harebells to woodlands and wetlands which, with our grasslands and fields, are our carbon sinks, our local or bioregional 'rainforest'.[2] We cherish our bio-regions by living sustainably locally which, with decreased trade and transport is the way we, in our supportive ecosystems, can reduce CO_2e emissions, begin to restabilise climate, restore soil and water, and live in a modest economy of quality, not growth. Living sustainably locally, without indefinite 'sustainable economic growth', however, differs from the way our dominant culture, even in droughts and winter floods, tends to proceed. Jewish scholar Jonathan Gorsky observes, 'Road building and airport expansion continue to provide tangible evidence of the power of short-term market forces to derail environmental good intentions.'[3] Comparing earth to a fragile living entity, from which people are taking too much, Jim Lovelock comments, 'We are taking so much that it is no longer able to sustain the familiar and comfortable world we have taken for granted. Now it is changing, according to its own internal rules to a state where we are no longer welcome.'[4]

To be welcome at home on earth again we need urgently to diminish demands on our finite planet and to reinhabit the earth community in co-operative symbiosis, in community with other people and all other creatures. We need to re-enter creation as fellow creatures with other animals, with plants, insects, aquatic life, and life's biodiverse support systems, in brief, as kin with sister and brother creatures, not as semi-detached exploiters indulging in non-renewable, climate damaging energies. The hour is late – some, with Lovelock, say too late – because we have not adequately

2. Graham Harvey, 'Fields of Carbon', *Living Earth* (Autumn 2009), pp.16-19.
3. Jonathan Gorsky, 'Judaic Models of Sacral Transformation', *Faiths in Creation* (London: Heythrop Institute for Religion, Ethics, and Public Life, 2008), p 15.
4. *The Revenge of Gaia*, p 7.

persuaded urban industrial people in developed regions, or people in aspirant developing regions, that unless we change course
immediately to more renewable energies and local sustainable
lifestyles, our children will be at planetary death's door. After ac-
cepting the Nobel Prize, Al Gore noted the depths of denial, and
how much needs to be done, and done quickly. 'Our grandchild-
ren', Gore said, 'will ask us one of two questions. Either they will
ask, "How could you have let this happen? Why didn't you do
something?" Or they will ask instead, "How did you manage to
do it? How did you succeed when so many said it was impossi-
ble?"' Unmentioned by Gore, however, but remarked by many,
including climate scientist James Hansen, is Gore's own carbon
intense car and air miles. All of us, quite literally, must walk, and
especially not fly, our talk! Also moved by the plight of children,
Drew Dellinger writes:

> it's 3.23 in the morning
> and I'm awake
> because my great great grandchildren
> won't let me sleep
> my great great grandchildren
> ask me in dreams
> what did you do while the planet was plundered?
> what did you do when the earth was unraveling?
>
> surely you did something
> when the seasons started failing?
> as the mammals, reptiles, birds were all dying?
>
> did you fill the streets with protest
> when democracy was stolen?
>
> what did you do
> once
> you
> knew?.....[5]

---

5. 'hieroglyphic stairway', www.drewdellinger.org

On Being Humbly Prophetic

Scripture's environmental laws are imaginative and helpful, they teach, sensitise, instruct, and educate, but laws take time to form the whole person and challenge an entrenched culture. Biblical laws, norms and customs generate a culture of 'don't waste', 'don't harm', and community, but they take time. And we're in overtime! Nor in our edge of 'climate chaos' can we afford time for any pedagogic and sensitising influences there may be in 'cap and trade', 'carbon allowances', and other business as usual devices to move our culture to mitigate climate change and live in 'climate justice'. Jewish, Christian and Moslem communities, including their sensitising laws, are minority movements within pluralist and individualising societies. Even were there time for Judaeo-Christian and Moslem norms of ecological justice to moderate contemporary culture, we are minorities, with other faiths, within our culture.

Prophecy is another matter. We can – and must – provide prophetic alternatives to individualised, consumer, globalised, 'growth' economies which are destroying the earth. Being prophetic, therefore, is more than predicting what will happen if our economies continue to consume, grow and destroy, or to aspire to same. Prophecy is more even than being God's spokespersons. Prophecy offers, promotes, and is a viable alternative to the assumptions and lifestyles of errant dominant cultures. In words of biblical scholar Walter Brueggemann, 'the task of prophetic ministry is to nourish and evoke a consciousness and perception alternative to the consciousness and perception of the dominant culture around us.'[6]

Prophetic ministry challenges even the prophets, as we noticed it challenges Al Gore, whose prophetic '*An Inconvenient Truth*' moved millions. Dominant cultures resist prophetic alternatives, sometimes lethally. Yet as a foremost prophet of last century, Barbara Ward, said, no society can long endure if it does not heed its prophets and wise persons. Our own dominant culture has, even after the publicity surrounding the Copenhagen

6. Walter Brueggemann, *The Prophetic Imagination* (Philadelphia: Fortress, 1978), p 13.

summit and its aftermath, ignored our prophets, including Barbara Ward, Rachel Carson, F. W. Schumacher, John Seymour, Patriarch Bartholomew, Archbishop Rowan Williams, Jonathon Porritt, James Hansen and not a few others, including Pope John Paul II in his prophetic call for 'an ecological conversion'. Prophecy is more even than contradicting the deleterious assumptions of our dominant culture, described by prophetic economist Paul Ekins, 'the possession and use of an increasing variety of goods and services is the principal cultural aspiration and the surest perceived route to personal happiness, social status, and national success.' Prophecy includes being prophetic alternatives in all our 'ways of proceeding', to adopt a favourite phrase of Ignatius Loyola, himself a prophetic alternative in his sixteenth century Spanish culture. Visitors from developed consumer societies are often delighted to discover in relatively rural and 're-mote' places (including places and subcultures in the EU, UK and Ireland) cultures integrated with their soil and biodiversity, food secure, and relatively self sufficient. Yet as we know from the experience of rural Ireland and Eastern Europe, many of these relatively secure communities are susceptible to western advertising, including Boxing Day furniture sales, shiny cars, large bungalows, and low cost airline holidays. As Eastern Europe, with its culture of sustainable family farmers and rural communities rushed to urbanise and join the consumerist EU, a young man in a Budapest bar spoke for many Eastern Europeans and developing peoples to journalist Alan Durning: 'People in the West think that we in Hungary don't know how they live. Well, we do know how they live, and we want to live like that too.'[7] Durning suggests, as the one hope for durable quality of life with food security, a value change alternative to the fateful aspirations of young people in Budapest, and other urban bars:

> The global environment cannot support 1.1 billion of us living like American consumers, much less 5.5 billion people, or a future population of at least 8 billion. On the other hand, reducing the consumption levels of the consumer society, and

7. In Alan Thein Durning, *How Much is Enough? The Consumer Society and the Future of the Earth* (London: Earthscan, 1992), p 35.

tempering material aspirations elsewhere, though morally acceptable, is a quixotic proposal. It bucks the trend of centuries. Yet it may be the only option ... Scientific advances, better laws, restructured industries, new treaties, environmental taxes, grassroots campaigns – all can help us get there. But ultimately, sustaining the environment that sustains humanity will require that we change our values.[8]

In possibly the most widely seen and heard speech in history, Barack Obama's inaugural address, now with John F. Kennedy's inaugural and Abraham Lincoln's second inaugural, included among America's inaugural classics, there were two intriguing, almost unnoticed passages which if genuinely heard, heeded and lived would prophetically challenge contemporary consumerist aspirations. Obama dared to mention, cautiously, what Americans do not like to hear: their disproportionate and unsustainable consumption of the earth's gifts, and the necessity to change lifestyles: 'We can no longer afford indifference to suffering outside our borders, nor can we consume the world's resources without regard to effect. For the world has changed, and we must change with it.' Here, worthy of our imitation, was a quiet countercultural challenge to the endless frontier, infinite resources illusion that has propelled the American dream, and now threatens to destroy it, and much else with it. Also buried in Obama's speech was a sensitive passage about sharing with one another, antithetical to market driven competitive consumerism: 'It is the kindness to take a stranger in when the levees break, the selflessness of workers who would rather cut their hours than see a friend lose their job which sees us through our darkest hours.' To shelter strangers and share work in difficult times – these illustrate the alternatives we can offer to competitive individualist cultures, including those which resent such suggestions. Far from the Potomac, in an interesting experiment in urban Scotland, Fiona Houston witnessed to her prophetic ideal based on 18th century rural peasant life, living for a year sharing meals with strangers while living on £20 a week.[9] In

8. Ibid., p 25.
9. Fiona Houston, *The Garden Cottage Diaries: My Year in the Eighteenth Century* (Edinburgh: Saraband, 2009).

its small, imaginative ways Houston's enacted witness recalls the alternative way Jesus shared meals with disciples and strangers 'from east and west'. In our own distinctive ways we can follow Houston's example and that of other prophetic persons, seeking alternatives and sharing even in urban settings as did the first Jerusalem Christians (Acts 2:44-47).[10]

As followers of Jesus, in communion with the first Christians and with contemporaries like Houston, Jeremy Williams, and the Lifestyle Movement, we anticipate the fuller coming of God's kingdom by preparing for it now, sharing the soil community in which we live, the food, water and climate, and by healing suffering in our local biosphere. Sharing the earth justly and healing suffering includes burying our dead, returning them with gratitude to the soil, including not only family and human friends, but strangers and pets and other animals who have shared our homes, gardens, and hearts in our anticipation of the peaceable kingdom. Another example, this time unlike Houston and Williams, a very rural and Gallican one, is that provided by Philip Oyler's description of an economy which is a delightful and sustainable alternative:

> The vintage, or *les vendanges* as it is called, lasts from the middle of September to the middle of October in the Dordogne valley. Some peasant or other will be busy picking each day, so if one is so disposed, one can pick (and eat!) grapes every day by helping different people. It would not be necessary to give a hand. One could walk round these vineyards, stop and have a chat with any of the little groups and be invited at once to help oneself to grapes or figs or anything else. When life is not on a purely financial basis, there is always time for a chat, for time is not reckoned as money, and a desire to share the good things of the earth shows itself in each and all. It is quite impossible to go into any peasant's home (or so I have found it) without being asked within two minutes to have something to eat or drink, no matter what time of day.[11]

10. Jeremy Williams, 'God, Monsters, and the Promise of Life', *Green Christian* 68 (Winter 2009/10), pp 6-8.

11. Philip Oyler, *The Generous Earth, An Account of Life in the Dordogne Valley in France, The Land of All Good Things* (London: Penguin, 1961), p 105.

Today, however, at least half of us live in relatively large settlements with earth crushing roads, airports, car parks, industries, shops, and dwellings on shrinking arable land. We also confront the problem of too many people making too many demands on our limited earth.[12] As we saw in that Budapest bar, many, perhaps most of us take as our role model infinite resource and growth driven North America. California economist Steven Blank is, with other economists, sometimes quoted as an example of denial of limits. Blank advises fellow Americans to abandon farming, move to cities, and enjoy globalised imports. Farming, he says, is not a necessity, at least for America, but 'a lifestyle choice'. Food, he says, can be produced everywhere, 'the whole world can do it'. Americans should become 'citizens of the world' and let other cultures produce food for Americans, while Americans parade their wealth and know-how for the future.[13] Blank, and flat earth climate change deniers notwithstanding we must, like Fiona Houston, Christian Ecology Link, Philip Oyler and many other people, find a variety of ways to re-enter creation sustainably both in large and small settlements and in smaller holdings. In brief, even in our time of migrations we can adapt the wisdom of Distributionism – to each person responsibility for a 'little land', even if merely a 'square foot garden', or window ledge, roof garden, or corner of nearby park or verge, recognising that at least for the medium term billions of people will live in conurbations or large settlements. Some cities already provide examples of relative sustainability, including Freiburg, Curitiba, and Chattanooga. In Freiburg, Germany, for example, most journeys are by bike or shared transport. Many homes are powered by solar or wind power. Some use just 150 kWh a year. In a new part of the city, Vauban, there are 120 cars for a thousand people, the EU average being about 600. A principal argument for another ruinous runway at once lush and fertile Heathrow was the need 'to be compet-

12. John Guillebaud, 'Two sides of the same coin', *Green Christian*, 65 (Summer 2008), pp 8-10; Edward Echlin, 'Cosmic relationships for a full Earth', Ibid., p 11.
13. Steven C. Blank, 'The End of the American Farm', *The Futurement* (April 1999), pp 25-27.

itive in a competitive world.' On the contrary, however, 'economic activity' henceforth must be non-competitive and sharing, with quality of life for people and the whole earth community. The Christian tradition of sharing, in imitation of Jesus' alternative lifestyle, and of the Christian ascetic tradition, can assist us to 'choose life' not 'growth'. In a visit to the Brazilian and Guianan Amazon, British Jesuit provincial, Michael Holman, witnessing the suffering of indigenous people from rapacious exploiting of the forest, had what he describes as a conversion experience. Like many Christians today from an athroposolic 'justice and peace' background, he realised what Christian ecology has long been saying, that we cannot separate people from our earth, and that in human suffering caused by exploitation of the earth the poor suffer most. Holman now wants not only the British Province but the worldwide Society of Jesus to use its gifts to care for creation. This, surely, is 'the greater glory of God', the 'magis' of today. Holman says:

> The worldwide Society of Jesus is adopting a seven year plan for generational change. The 19,000 Jesuits throughout the world, along with those for whom and with whom we work, are being asked to identify specific ways in which they will live more responsibly and lead others to do the same. The Society's project embraces retreat centres and schools and universities, social centres and research as well as personal and communal lifestyles. We are being encouraged to live and work in an ecologically sensitive way, to inspire all students to commit themselves to the environment, to write on the spiritualities and theology of creation and to use our media centres to publicise successful initiatives.[14]

The day Holman's testimony was published there was a service at Methodist Central Hall, Westminster, at which the Archbishops of Canterbury and Westminster spoke on the Christian responsibility to care for creation, after which tens of thousands walked to Westminster to encourage leaders to act

---

14. Michael Holman, 'The Amazon Changed Me', *The Tablet* (5 December 2009), p 11.

generously at the Copenhagen summit and thereafter. From a Moslem perspective, Markbul Rahim also proposes an alternative to exploitative growth economy:

> The ultimate and basic purpose of economic production does not consist in the increase of goods produced, nor in profit, nor in prestige; it is directed to the service of man, that is of man in his totality, taking into account his material needs and the requirements of his intellectual, moral, spiritual and religious life ... humanity and the universe and all in it are a part of the creation of God to fulfil the purpose of creation. This is to worship God through living life on earth in accordance with his guidance. Ownership of all things is with Allah, the Creator and Sustainer.[15]

Christians – and other faiths – can resonate with these words. The earth with all its gifts is God's. As Christopher Wright notes, 'the most explicit assertion of Divine land ownership in the Old Testament is made for the sake of protecting the family and its land.'[16] We, with the land entrusted to us, glorify God by caring for the land and its climate and sharing all earth's gifts with our fellow creatures. The charities to which we contribute, and even the bird feeder in our gardens or on a window ledge, symbolise our sharing with fellow creatures and with them glorifying God. The shoppers' mall is a lonely temple. The quality of life, indeed life itself (*multum*), transcends the quantity of shopping, acquisitions, 'growth' and material 'progress' (*multa*). In a quality economy, hope in eternal life with other creatures, and preparing for that awaited kingdom now is, to say the least, countercultural to secular humanism. Inner and community peace include appreciation of the fragile beauty and biodiversity of earth, in faith and trust in Holy Mystery. Richard St Barbe-Baker speaks more sensitively and perceptively than growth economics, even 'low carbon' economics: 'You can gauge a country's wealth, its real wealth, by its tree cover.'

15. Makbul Rahim, 'A Faith Perspective on the Economy', *Faiths in Creation*, pp 40-41.

16. Christopher J. H. Wright, *God's People in God's Land, Family, Land, and Property in the Old Testament* (Grand Rapids: Pater Noster Press, 1997), p 65.

Homes and a Prophetic Alternative

Suddenly, to my awareness at least, our homes – the built environments in which we dwell – have become, to paraphrase Marshall McLuhan, a significant part of the medium of the prophetic alternative message. Journalists have investigated – and reported – the energy use of some high profile environmentalists. There have even been unattributed 'leaks' of fuel bills, including 'air conditioning'! Some bishops have recognised that their residences send a message and have moved to modest homes in the midst. Approximately a quarter of CO_2 emissions in developed regions come from homes. If we are to reduce emissions by 40% or more by 2020, we must 'revisit' our own homes. We can remind ourselves that house, and still less bungalow, is not a univocal description of a human dwelling. Home can be a modern house, a bungalow, or terrace, for some a flat, a bedsit, a room or communal residence, sheltered accommodation, a care home, perhaps a park bench, even temporarily a warm pavement. Homes can be humble, and lonely. Significantly, in a local park, where residents sometimes – and very expensively! – dedicate memorial trees, someone recently dedicated a tree 'to those who died alone'. In a Jesuit secondary school where I once taught, a group of teens called 'the Aramathea group' serve as volunteer pall bearers for people who die alone, 'unwept, unhonoured, and unsung'. Significantly, if much less poignantly, a specialist on zero carbon homes recently illustrated a lecture by slides of various zero carbon homes he had adapted. They ranged from a 'new build' six bedroom mansion to a modest Victorian terrace converted to zero carbon. His lecture illustrated our point: home is not a univocal concept, although the old saying remains true, 'there's no place like home'. Each of us can adapt as much as possible our own home, whether large or humble, to the zero carbon ideal.

Some countries, led by Germany, are building mostly zero carbon homes and adapting existing ones. Fundamental to zero or low carbon is insulation. Or as that zero carbon specialist said – 'insulate, insulate, insulate'. He suggested double glazing, thick adjustable curtains that can be opened when winter sun is shining

– to welcome 'passive solar' heat and light – and closed when it is dark. In well insulated buildings passive solar, especially when combined with body heat and lights, sometimes provides all the necessary warmth even on cold winter days. Specialists also recommend draught proofed doors, with thick moveable curtains. Lofts are especially important. That speaker and his colleagues recommend treated sheep wool for lofts, which also assists sheep farmers. I once met a woman fell walker collecting wool caught on fences and hedges which she added to her loft insulation! I also know people who recycle worn woollen jumpers as insulation. Walls and floors must be insulated in ways appropriate to one's home. A carpet specialist and neighbour, Den Parkinson, recommends wool carpets. Thankfully, local authorities now provide grants for loft and wall insulation. Shared party walls and outside walls facing south or west have suddenly become energy saving luxuries.

To reduce emissions by 40% or more by 2020, we need the impressive variety of alternative energies, produced by 'green jobs'. The UK, with its surprising wealth of winds, tides, waves, lagoons, air and ground thermal and biomass potential, and solar energies especially near the south and east coasts, should soon be able to enjoy an alternative, sustainable economy without nuclear or coal power. Unfortunately, Britain has suffered from successive parliaments infatuated with nuclear power and, despite its enormous potential for alternatives, still lags behind other EU nations in 'good energy'. Nevertheless alternatives are now appearing on roofs and near homes and other buildings. Solar generation is visibly increasing near coasts and in other relatively 'hot spots'. We have had solar thermal, installed by a local firm, for fourteen years which heats our water from April through October, and boosts it even in dark winter! Our fourteen photovoltaic panels, installed by nearby Chelsfield Solar on our south facing roof, produce more electricity than we use, the remainder entering the grid, making us one of an increasing array of micro-generators. Our electricity company, recommended by Operation Noah and Friends of the Earth, is Good Energy, which supplies only renewably sourced energy, and pays us for what we produce, including what we use.

Solar installation takes a while to recover the initial capital outlay even with grants, but that capital investment returns more than it would invested elsewhere, and government feed-in tariffs, as in Germany, are beginning. More importantly, solar panels reduce our own and UK carbon footprints, increase the value of homes, and fascinate people who like to view roofs. Churches too, blessed with their south facing roofs, can be micro-generators, a mini-gospel in every community they serve, and secure a steady income for the parish. As I write, my own parish community hopes to have panels installed which, once the initial outlay is made, will provide a better financial return than if the capital were invested elsewhere. And most important is the witness that panels provide.

Water harvesting is another prophetic alternative which can be used for plants, gardens, cleaning, showers, and sometimes toilets. Here in the often arid southeast we have butts at each of our three downpipes, each butt with its own subsidiary butt. Others, such as George and Joyce Dent of Andover, Hampshire, include underground cisterns. These are especially appropriate for spring and summer gardening. Abundant winter rain, when little harvested water is needed, can be returned to aquifers rather than wasted in drains. John Fowler of Farm Crisis Network, generously connects moveable hosepipes to butts, thereby returning water to the soil and aquifers even in winter. This is especially important where garden covering or 'ground construction' is fashionable.

The Garden Community
Water and soil lead us to gardens. In the UK an estimated 80% of 'old build' homes have one. We immediately remind ourselves, however, that for some that garden is a window ledge, a grow-bag, a few containers. For others a garden is literally an arable acre or more. If we inspect our own gardens, especially when we have recently moved, we sometimes notice 'ground construction' that we can remove by rolling back some inherited tiles, removing slabs, chipping away crescents around walls and planting wall trained fruit. It's also helpful to remove ground sterilising ley-

landii. Although non-productive plants and flowers are good for quality of life, atmosphere and climate, people are not limiting front gardens to these but are growing food in front too. In addition to an allotment-like rear garden on a four year rotation, supplanted by three partly raised beds on a three year rotation, I also catch crop vegetables in front. When an inherited elderly rose dies, I replace it with a soft fruit. I grow eight dwarfed pears in front, four as upright cordons on an east facing wall. I also grow Maypole and Waltz ballerina apples, a half standard gooseberry, a worcesterberry, and a blackberry in front. By using dwarfing root stock I'm able to grow about ninety fruit varieties, with over a hundred plants, counting a few strawberries, raspberries, and rhubarb.

What we said about varieties of homes also applies to gardens. Most can accommodate at least one or two 3x20 feet vegetable beds in relatively small gardens. Every tree or fruit plant in a conurbation contributes to food security and climate stabilisation, as does every parsley or chive in those window boxes. Every plant, like every garden slab *removed* helps, just as every perennial grass field or restored local woodland does. When teens from eco-clubs of our two local secondary schools addressed a Council cabinet meeting, both clubs requested the council to plant more trees. We can and should plant fruit and nut trees throughout our neighbourhoods. Verges, churches, schools, hospitals, flats and care homes generally have 'a little land' suitable for fresh – and local – fruit in season. My own church, for example, has a cherry plum, two ballerina apples, a rhubarb, pink currant, and a walnut, in addition to some welcome brambles feeding people and wildlife in the wildlife sanctuary corner. Most homes can and should reserve a garden corner for wildlife, including a small pond and bird feeder. Some with larger gardens accommodate a companionable suburban goat or some laying hens, including spent battery hens.[17] Food growing, with a wildlife corner, and sometimes a few animals or hens, is a superb way to reintegrate children with the earth and heal their 'nature deficit disorder'. Closely related is the major challenge to assist youth aged 13-35 to re-enter earth as creation – and church.

Much more urban food growing, including front and rear gar-

17. cf The Battery Hen Welfare Trust, 01769 580310.

dens, allotments, holdings, and farms, and more preserving for
the late winter, early spring 'hunger gap', is imperative if the
small, crowded island where I write is to survive climate related
catastrophe. According to a recent Soil Association estimate, the
UK is only 58% food self sufficient, versus 65% in 1980. That is a
frightening and ominous estimate. As carbon and other emissions
increase in the atmosphere, and as temperatures creep upwards,
food growing becomes more difficult. We learned from the 350
campaign before and since the Copenhagen meetings, and in
campaigning aimed at the UN summit in Mexico, that we must
reduce our CO_2 emissions so that there are at most 350 parts per
million in the atmosphere. It is well above that now, and has been
increasing by around 2% annually, partly through global food
trade. We recklessly import 90% of our fruit, most of our nuts, and
about half of our vegetables, with the inherent food insecurity,
climate damaging food and virtual water miles such dysfunctional
trade includes. Ominously less that 1% of the population is now
engaged in farming. As Alan Gear says, every farming family
which leaves the land is, and remains, an irreplaceable loss to the
country of experience, knowledge, skill and soil wisdom.
Meanwhile our dwindling arable fields suffer erosion from deforestation, intensive chemical agribusiness, link roads, bypasses,
runways, car parks, and soil devouring construction and ex-
urbanisation. The hypermarket supply chain, with its climate
damaging food miles, packaging, and exploitation of local growers, supplies around three quarters of UK food. Several recent
governments insisted that global trade makes us food secure.
Hence the carefree planning consents for roads, airports, and construction. Ministers and business leaders still insist that indefinite
'sustainable economic growth' is possible and desirable, even on
a relatively small if fertile island with temperatures – and waters –
rising. Ironically, the Heathrow airport sprawl was once among
the most fertile soil communities in Europe.

London requires around 8.5 million hectares to feed it, and is
threatened by flooding. London, even now, in other words, depends on a global hinterland, the countryside around other world
communities, to feed Londoners. Urgently, however, London

and settlements everywhere must restore, nurture and relate to their own urban soil, and the soil of their own hinterlands, if the billions in settlements are to stabilise climate and survive. London's peril will become more obvious if and when sea level rise engulfs East Anglian agricultural land and the London Thames barrier. Herbert Girardet says,

> Historically, many traditional cities grew and prospered by assuring sustainable supplies of food and forest products from the surrounding countryside. This is true of medieval European cities such as Siena or Dinkelsbuehl, with their concentric rings of market gardens, forests, orchards, farm and grazing land, as well as of many cities in Asia, where this practice continues today. Future cities can learn a great deal from this model, even if we cannot simply import traditional practices into the 21st century unchanged.[18]

Settlements, in other words, have prospered by utilising healthy hinterlands for food cultivation, orchards, woodland, mining, landfill, with the negative feedback that well cared for hinterlands provide. Even presently unsustainable London, which, as we noted, depends precariously on a global hinterland, can and must again live symbiotically, in a circular metabolism returning to the soil what is taken from the soil, utilising London's remaining precious inner green spaces and immediate hinterland. Girardet warns: 'Cities suck in resources and dump wastes in nature, and in an urbanising world it is crucial to create a better match between urban resource use and the world's ecosystems. The environmental impact of increasing urban resource use is becoming the dominant feature of the human presence on earth.'[19]

The Proximity Principle

We can rise to this challenge, securing our own and our children's future, by following the proximity principle, proposed by Sir Julian Rose, a Berkshire organic farmer and co-founder of the

---

18. Herbert Girardet, *Cities People Planet, Liveable Cities for a Sustainable World* (Chichester: John Wiley & Sons, 2004), p 19.
19. Ibid., p 89.

'Coalition to Protect the Polish Countryside', as 'a system that
ensures that full utilisation is made of the local resources base, before turning to areas further afield for the community's basic
needs.'[20] The proximity principle adapted by each settlement for its
unique situation, means we live symbiotically, in a circular
metabolism, with our own immediate countryside, supporting our
own farmers, traders and soil, which in turn supports, feeds and
clothes us. It is immensely important that we encourage developing
regions and people everywhere to follow the proximity principle,
sustaining and appreciating their own regional farmers and growers. I was profoundly moved by a recently published letter from a
Christian Oxfordshire farmer: 'For us farmers climate change is becoming a challenge not only because of temperature rise but also
longer periods of drought and intense rainfall. At the moment the
livestock sector is in deep crisis. Please keep praying for these farmers faced with extinction.'[21] Developing world, and eastern European
farmers also need these prayers, and for similar reasons.

Julian Rose notes that industrial agriculture, with intemperate
mining and burning of fossil fuels, leads to what he calls 'mutually
assured destruction'. When we live the proximity principle, however, we acquire most of our food, drinks, fabric and fuel from the
familiar soil community within and near our cities, towns and villages. There will be exceptions, including bananas, citrus, tea, coffee, cocoa and cotton – but we can acquire even these from as nearby
as possible, with as few air and ship miles as possible. We can assist and encourage 'developing' regions to implement their own
proximity principle, preserving their soil fertility, forests, virtual
water, biodiversity and bioregional support systems rather than
deforesting and intensifying. Aid agencies should not encourage
developing regions to grow cash crops for distant trade which ultimately damages the very people – and soil – they say they are
helping to 'develop'. The air and ship miles carbon intensive, re-
frigerated and packaged global trade culture is antithetical to the
prophetic alternative we must be.

20. Sir Julian Rose, 'The Proximity Principle', *Fourth World Review*
(September 2009), p 23.
21. In Echlin, 'Climate Change Theology', *New Blackfriars*, p 72.

Fortunately food production and consumption is an area where most people have real influence, especially when we act together and locally, as in home and community gardens, community supported agriculture, and farmers' markets and shops. Lord Peter Melchett of the Soil Association, a free range stock farmer, says that we all must eat less meat because the carbon footprint of intensive meat production is unsustainable. Thanks to Melchett, Graham Harvey, Alan Gear and dieticians we are learning it is more healthy and sustainable to eat perennial grass fed meat or grain direct, rather than grain fed meat. It impoverishes soil and people to grow soya and grain, especially if exported, for intensively reared animals. Intensively reared animals also emit disproportionate quantities of methane. Therefore when eating meat, eggs or dairy products, including in restaurants, we should eat only free range fowl and stock. The proximity principle includes knowing where and how our food originates.

It can be delightfully surprising how many local vineyards, orchards, breweries and distilleries we enjoy in northwest Europe. Bottled and canned drinks, including fruit juice and vinegar can be produced locally. We can eliminate air, ship and lorry emissions from transport of drinks that can be produced locally or at least regionally. Here in southeast England we're especially blessed in our variety of vineyards, orchards, hops and breweries. Indeed we keep discovering new ones! Especially popular in East Sussex is Oakwood Farm, near Robertsbridge, farmed by Matthew and Carol Wilson, which not only grows a variety of organic apples and pears but produces and blends organic fruit juices and cider. For whisky, brandy, and gin (not forgetting blackthorn hedgerows for sloe gin at Christmas), we can still follow the proximity principal by not going beyond the EU. For bourbon aficionados, sadly, Kentucky is many drink miles away! What we must especially avoid are imported 'new world wines', now flowing through the UK and Ireland. Recently in Ireland I found restaurants, shops and pubs awash with wine from the Andes, despite the recovering 'Celtic Tiger's' soaring CO_2e emissions, and the reasonable proximity of struggling French vintners, not to mention the indigenous 'dark stuff' called 'Arthur'. In the

UK, improving white, rosé and sparkling wines, some of them prize winners, now rival the continent. Vineyards are increasing, and France is not far away. The nearer the vineyards that supply us, the healthier the rural areas and growers, and the fewer wine miles.

Imported drink and food – and even flowers – contribute to the transfer of 'virtual water' from water stressed regions. Southern Spain averages only 430 mm of rainfall, versus the UK's 1400 mm. Yet many of the food insecure UK's food and drink imports come from rural Spain. We can assist Andalucia to follow the proximity principle by our example and by our importing from southern Europe and beyond only what cannot be grown here, such as olives, citrus, avocados, and occasionally red wines. An oft cited glaring example of dysfunctional trade in virtual water is northern Europe importing Kenyan flowers, while Kenya suffers deadly drought. Israel deprives Palestinians not only of their homes and olives but of water, in what is sometimes called another holocaust. We can avoid imports from the occupied West Bank, while demanding justice for the indigenous people there. Barbara Stocking, Chief Executive of Oxfam, says 'Trade with Israeli settlements – which are illegal under international law – contributes to their economic viability and serves to legitimate them. It is clear from our development work in West Bank communities that settlements lead to the denial of human rights and create poverty for Palestinians.'

Since 1985 the UK has suffered the loss of many hedgerow habitats, a diminishment of native bird species and of species rich meadows, erosion of top soil, an estimated 15,000 farmers a year leaving the land and, until the recent resurgence, a decline in family gardens. By supporting local farmers and growers, and by encouraging Eastern Europe and developing nations to cherish small and family farms, we are a prophetic alternative to agribusiness, the GMO lobby, the WTO, World Bank, and growth economics. Poland, for example, before joining the EU enjoyed 1.5 million family farms of around 18 acres, providing a sustainable quality of life in that beautiful countryside for 20% of the working population and families. The EU encouraged Polish farmers to abandon farming for urban industries 'to improve their economic position'. Remaining farmers were encouraged to intensify and 'be competitive' with western European agribusiness. Many young people have deserted farming and Polish rural life, for what they consider the wealth of the urban west. The EU policy also succeeded in Portugal, where 60% of small farmers, like their UK predecessors, left the land or 'became extinct' in the words of the Oxfordshire farmer quoted above. Eastern and western Europe, Africa, and parts of Asia, especially China, busily destroying its sustainable rural culture, need counter cultural alternatives encouraging them to preserve their farms and homes, with their biodiversity, history and fertile fields, and to appreciate quality and sharing on the land, in preference to pursuit of consumerist utopias.

A prophetic movement in Fife, Scotland, surprisingly boasts 'the Fife Diet' of food and drink mostly from Fife itself. The Fife Diet boasts local produce which southerners could envy, including a wide range of seafood, cereals, meat and dairy products, vegetables, and top and soft fruit. The Fife Diet, like those everywhere, occasionally reaches beyond borders for locally inaccessible foods and drink – but not for malt whiskies! Near where I write in the southern UK, in East Sussex, Elizabeth and Andrew Gorsuch, following Fife's initiative, promote a Kent and Sussex diet. Surprisingly for the relatively lush southeast, there are few cereals like oats and wheat grown locally, therefore the Kent and Sussex diet includes some breakfast foods and flour imported from nearby in the UK. A wide variety of local foods, beers and wines abound, however, within the home counties, although tropical fruits, and tea, coffee, chocolate, and rice are imported, as is Scotch whisky – from Fife! The Gorsuch diet permits 20% imports, but for that 20% follows the proximity principal and buys organic.

In Depth Holidays

All living creatures deserve their rest and Sabbath. In the Jubilee tradition, familiar to Jesus, even the soil rested. Humans are no exception. 'Rest and relaxation' holidays can be earth friendly, low carbon and sustainable when they adhere to what we call the 'in depth principle' closely related to the proximity principle. As currently promoted by tour-preneurs and airlines, including some 'fly and sail' sea voyages, holidays are a major contributor to greenhouse gases. Following the 'in depth principle' we can enjoy 'sabbaths' where we live, experiencing bioregional and cultural depth rather than skimming or flying along the surface. This is true of 'new world' people too. Americans, for example, have fifty fascinating states, with their ecology and history, in addition to the myriad other treasures within the western hemisphere. Similarly, people living in northern Europe could spend a lifetime – or several – experiencing some of the cultural and historical places in their own countries, and in Europe itself, and still barely scratch the surface of the depth near their doorstep. For anyone living in the UK, holidays in England, Wales, Scotland and the Isles, as well as Ireland and the continent could occupy many life-times without distant travel. People who practice the 'in depth principle' report their astonishment at the depth of history, art, architecture, and the natural world in their own home counties, let alone their whole country, or their wider bioregion.

Holiday firms offer 'eco-tourism' in interesting (because distant) places. Some, such as the Galapagos and Antarctica may be interesting. But as Barbara Ward asked, 'If everyone goes to the same beauty spot, what beauty will there be left to see?' or what wildlife? Certainly it is better on exotic holidays to eat local mangoes rather than 'fish and chips' imported from Europe. It is better still to encourage people everywhere to follow the proximity and in depth principles, appreciating and conserving their own bioregional resources rather than neglecting what is near for a supposedly preferable exotic afar. In Sussex a local environment group promotes holidays in local 'hot spots', especially interesting places, while discouraging long haul visitors from the New South Wales and New York jetting fraternities. Hopefully the latter will soon, rather than too late, discover the depths of their own regions.

Children

The importance of encouraging children to mature into genuine alternatives to the unsustainable culture threatening their future cannot be overstated. Rather than grooming them into a culture of self-destructive denial, we owe it to God and them to assist children to enter a quality culture of living sustainably locally. Their innate affinity with plants and animals should be fostered. Pets and gardens are a way into the wider soil community for urban children. Parents, teachers, carers and extended families can introduce them to green fields and rural areas, to trees and woodlands and wildlife, to museums and galleries. As early in life as practical, they should be introduced to the production of local, organic, free range food.[22] They should be encouraged, as many now are, to practice the 'three Rs' of reduce, re-use, recycle – and also to refuse and repair. Children enjoy composting, harvesting rain water, and appreciate alternative energies. Ruth Jarman, Board member of Operation Noah, not only attuned her three children to the natural world, but takes them with her on climate demonstrations. She and her oldest daughter Helen took the 36 hour train trip to Copenhagen to demonstrate – for children's and the earth's future – with 100,000 people 'who know how bad things are, believe there is still hope for the earth, and cannot but act on that hope'. Helen celebrated her tenth birthday on the train somewhere in Denmark. Ruth says, 'She has some understanding of the place of her generation in history. She said to me the other day "You're so lucky, Mummy, you are probably living in the best time ever – you haven't lived through a war and climate change hasn't happened yet for you. But it will for me".'

In addition to vibrant eco-clubs, pupils deserve a whole eco-school community striving to keep their school low carbon and sustainable. The environment should be included in all courses, whether science, humanities, or vocational. Religious education remains of paramount importance. For example, during the Darwin anniversary commemoration (2009), Sir David Attenborough did, and repeated, a prime time television special on Charles Darwin. Unfortunately, Attenborough displayed a confident ignorance of the Bible as literature, and of its literary forms, delighting in portraying it as naïve history and science, and therefore wrong.

22. Caroline Mills, 'Little Helpers', *Grow It* (March 2009). pp 50-53; Tim Jacques, 'Dads on the Plot', *Organic Way* (Spring 2009), pp 14-15.

Darwin himself, as we noticed above, was less confident and more nuanced. Children deserve to be taught – as Attenborough and Richard Dawkins deserved to be taught – that in William Blake's words, the Bible is 'full of pictures', profound truths communicated through literature.

Every school, college, university – even every day-care centre – like every chapel, temple, synagogue, and mosque, should be a sustainable centre within the local community, surrounded by trees and plants, radiating human communion, under God, with the earth. Whether we are parents, teachers, relatives or simply friends and fellow citizens, all of us are challenged to foster earth literacy among children, so that they may persevere into their teens and beyond. Closely related to earth literacy is the challenge to perseverance in church attendance, with the unique church life and witness earth literate young people bring.

The Christian Prophetic Alternative

As Jesus was a prophetic alternative to the imperial and Herodian economies, so we, Jesus as community today, are countercultural to our own dominant acquisitive and 'growth' economies. I believe that a principal reason that churches make so little impact on contemporary culture is what I call 'forgetfulness of Christ'. We easily become so obsessed with 'the church' as structures, ministers, orientation, and with inward journeying spiritualities, that we sometimes forget that we are the prophetic presence of the living and risen Jesus Christ. We may wonder what the itinerant Jesus, with his sharing and agrarian lifestyle, and his preaching of an active hope in the kingdom, would think of the Pope's new red shoes, of parishes closing for lack of compulsorily celibate priests, and of jet holidaying religious. To be Jesus Christ as community today, we must rediscover the evolutive Christ, finding him in all things, as Ignatius Loyola and, in our times, Père Teilhard did. We can repent by changing our values and practices, becoming ministers to people and the whole earth community.

That means our homilies and catechesis, and all religious instruction and practical witness, must be worthy of Christ's followers, his presence on earth today. Ministry of the word requires more study and better preparation, with better presentation, than is often found. Service of the word demands prayer and practice, in brief ministry worthy of Jesus. Responsible ministry includes continuing education and study for as long as a minister serves God's word and God's people. At our time of climate change, food and water insecurity, and biodiversity loss, ecologically and theologically informed ministry is necessary. Lay people too, including parents and all members of the Christian family, share in the privilege of bringing Christ to people and their earth. Many lay people and ordained ministers find theology group reading and discussions, 'lectio-divina', reading and contemplating the Bible imaginatively, and, for ministers, group homily preparations, helpful.[23]

Rites of Passage

In baptism we become, as it were, saturated with Christ, we are so united with him and with each other that we are Christ as community today. The priestly ministry of all baptised Christians means we, who are Christ as community, serve our fellow creatures leading them in cosmic worship. Our baptismal commission empowers us to become a prophetic priestly alternative and witness to our culture which is in denial of both God's reconciling presence in Jesus and the fragility of creation. We can relate our baptismal and eucharist services to forests and trees, especially the Golgotha tree. Every church and chapel deserves a baptismal tree to which children and ministers can return baptismal and other sacramental water. A good example is St Mary's and St John's 'living churchyard' in Oxford, with its Blenheim Orange apple tree, native to Oxfordshire, to which children return sacred water. In my churchyard parents, with two children present, planted a cherry plum, a traditional local hedgerow tree, to which children and servers return water. This beautiful practice symbolises that Christians are water and tree people, an earth renewing presence wherever they live and worship.

23. Chris Hayden, 'Lectio Divina: The Challenge in Parish and Pastoral Settings', in *Reading Scripture for Living the Christian Life*, Bernard Treacy OP, ed (Dublin: Dominican Publications, 2009), pp 47-56.

Closely related to baptism and the eucharist is the rite of strengthening, or confirmation in the Holy Spirit. To be the reconciling Christ in climate chaos will demand strength and courage, as in Christian ecological leaders it already does. Confirmation strengthens us, in Christ, for the service of renewing and preserving the earth for future generations. In Michigan, the native Americans regard themselves not as 'owners' but as keepers of the earth for future generations in a culture similar to today's Christian environmentalists. Ottawa elder, Jimmie Mitchell, for example, explains: 'In our belief we only own what we can carry to the other side of this existence. Ownership is not what we feel about our homelands. We revere the earth as our Mother to epitomise our connection to her. She provides for us, and in respect we take care to ensure she remains wholesome and viable for seven generations.' Another prominent Ottawa, Hank Bailey, is a conservationist with a special interest in trees, whose great great grandfather cried when signing over native lands to white 'ownership' in 1836. Bailey says, 'We are the keepers of the seven generations. Our ancestors are watching to see if we make a life for those yet unborn and teach the care of our Mother Earth to all races of men.'[24]

In the UK 'keepers of the seven generations' require the strength of confirmation as they contend with road, airport, nuclear, GMO, coal, oil, agribusiness and other lobbies who live only for their own generation disregarding the future. Christopher Strangeways, prominent Rye organic farmer and conservationist, and a leader of Rother Environment Group (REG) speaks for many who care about 'the seven generations' when he says he is 'saddened' that so many good and well meaning people have been misled by the nuclear lobby. Investment in nuclear has deprived safer and better alternative energies of billions including inestimable brain hours of scientific research and development. The rite of confirmation strengthens Christians to protect what is right, good and

24. Todd Spencer, 'Where Sustainability Comes From', *Traverse* (November 2008), pp 38-39; cf Colin Taylor and William C. Sturtevant, *The Native Americans The Indigenous People of North America* (NY: Smithmark, 1996), pp 472-486.

sustainable. Lester Brown, President of the Earth Policy Institute, describes the challenge confronting us:

> Amory B. Lovins and Imtan Sheikh put the cost of electricity from a new nuclear power plant at 14 cents per kilowatt hour and that from wind power at 7 cents per kilowatt hour. This comparison includes the costs of fuel, capital, operation and maintenance, and transmission and distribution. It does not include the additional costs for nuclear of disposing of waste, insuring plants against an accident, and decommissioning the plants when they wear out. Given the huge gap, the so-called nuclear revival can succeed only by unloading these costs onto taxpayers. If all the costs of generating nuclear are included in the price to consumers, nuclear power is dead in the waters ... Though nuclear power plants are still being built in some countries and governments are talking them up in others, the reality is that we are entering the age of wind, solar, and geothermal energy.[25]

Nevertheless – and this especially is the challenge for which confirmation strengthens us – pro-nuclear interests in industry, the media, and as Brown notes, in some governments including the UK, persist in promoting nuclear as essential to 'the mix'. Other lobbies are similarly challenging.

United with Christ and each other in baptism, and strengthened in the Holy Spirit in confirmation, we re-present in the eucharist a memorial of Christ's last hours in which he offered to God, his Father, the cosmos radically reconciled in his incarnation. When at our eucharist we recall 'the everlasting covenant', offering the cosmos in Christ to God, we recall the inclusive Noachic covenant, in words repeated in the Letter to the Hebrews, and now in our eucharist (Gen 9:16; Heb 13:20). Through 'bread which earth has given and human hands have made' and 'wine fruit of the vine and work of human hands', we offer the whole cosmos 'through, with, and in him'. As baptised and confirmed people, especially at the eucharist we lead all earth creatures in

25. Lester Brown, 'The Flawed Economics of Nuclear Power', *Spirit Earth* (February 2009), p 6.

praise of our shared Creator as we say, 'all creation rightly gives you praise'. Our eucharists, therefore, include the whole earth community, ourselves and our 'cosmic covenant' partners. We petition the Holy Spirit to make our offerings of the earth 'holy', that as reconciled and inter-related with Jesus through his incarnation, they may symbolise his presence within the earth today. Our eucharists also symbolise and contain our own self offering, our *kenosis*, in reconciling, earth-inclusive lives as Jesus Christ today.

The eucharist deepens the awareness of communicants that Christians are a eucharistic community. Gathering, after the eucharist, for coffee or conversation is appropriate for a eucharistic community. So too are frequent shared meals. Jesus gave an example in his frequent communal meals with his followers, some of the meals outdoors, as did the first Christians in 'breaking the bread' in their homes. Shared meals are an important part of Christian alternative living. The American Green Sisters give three useful guidelines: 1) When we eat together, share only 'ethical' food, free of chemicals, GMOs, and intensification; 2) share only local cultivated food; 3) share meals in gratitude to God our Creator.[26] Timothy Gorringe relates the eucharist to shared meals, and both to the centrality of food, 'The fact that the eucharist is the central act of Christian worship follows in part from the fact that table fellowship was a central part of Jesus' life and ministry. Concern with food, then, is as central to our liturgy as it is to our daily life.'[27]

We also share reconciliation rites, including admission of faults at the eucharist. We should include ecological sins which damage earth life and habitats, including unnecessary car and air transport which is a paramount example of earth and climate damage. Even electric cars require acres of asphalt for roads and parking spaces. Reconciliation for ecological failings includes imaginative reparation for what damage we may have done, and

26. Sarah McFarland Taylor, *Green Sisters, A Spiritual Ecology* (London: Harvard University Press, 2007), p 163.

27. Timothy Gorringe, *Harvest, Food, Farming and the Churches* (London: SPCK, 2006), p 74.

the resolution to change our actions. The 'weeks of reparation' in parishes last century were imaginative. Perhaps families could adapt the ancient Lenten Wednesday and Friday abstinence from meat to exclude all intensively reared or imported meat and dairy products and sea creatures. Establishing wilderness sanctuaries in our gardens and churchyards makes reparation, as does planting throughout settlements insect friendly trees and plants which nurture and shelter fellow creatures. The same is true of bird houses and feeders, and wildlife ponds.

Closely associated with reconciliation services and reparation is the rite of unction, anointing with oil of seriously sick and dying members of the community. We are recovering the community nature of 'extreme unction' or 'the sacrament of the severely sick', as it was in the early church. The letter of James illustrates the community dimension of anointing:

> Is any one among you suffering? Let him pray. Is any cheerful? Let him sing praise. Is any among you sick? Let him call for the elders of the church, and let them pray over him, anointing him with oil in the name of the Lord; and the prayer of faith will save the sick man, and the Lord will raise him up; and if he has committed sins, he will be forgiven (Jas 5:13-15).

Even today in Eastern churches sometimes as many as six 'elders of the church' administer anointing. In the west we have communal anointings in hospitals, hospices, and homes. Priests, deacons, ministers and other baptised people participate. Olive oil, usually blessed by a bishop on Maundy Thursday, or oil from a local plant, is used to anoint the 'five senses'. Anointing, which is sometimes followed by bodily healing, reminds us of our relationships with other earth creatures, that we are inconceivable without our soil community which daily we see, hear, smell, and touch, that we too are soil creatures. Anointing of the sick never forgets the inevitable death, and the life which follows death, as in the western rite prayer, 'May the Lord who frees you from sin save you and raise you up.' In death our bodies become what Karl Rahner called pancosmic, within the cosmos, with God, nourishing other creatures, awaiting personal resurrection in, with, and through Christ

risen. William Wordsworth vividly – and imaginatively – anticipated Rahner's pancosmic imagery when Wordsworth portrayed
the dead Lucy he loved, 'rolled round in earth's diurnal course,
with rocks and stones and trees.' Green burials especially symbolise our pancosmic presence and our shared hope in resurrection
when Jesus returns.[28]

Appropriately for God's people, who are Christ existing as
community today, our final two principal rites of passage are
communal: holy orders and matrimony. In holy orders, or ordination, we publicly commission and recognise men and women to
lead our worship, preside at our eucharists, serve as centres of
unity and, in brief, to minister to us in word, sacrament, and pastoral care. An eighth century Gallican ordination rite expresses
our hope in our ministers: '... meditating day and night upon thy
law, O thou Almighty, what he readeth he may believe: what he
believeth, he may teach, what he teacheth, he may practice.'[29]
Priests, deacons, bishops, and other ministers teach and practice
Christian ecology.[30] Resistance to earth inclusion in ministerial
preparation and service is waning. We now rarely hear the neo-
dualist dismissal of Christian ecology 'this has nothing to do with
the church'. Nevertheless, theological societies, theological colleges, universities, and seminaries still need to be more earth inclusive, we might say more Christian. When in 2009, the year of the
Copenhagen summit, the European Society of Catholic Theology
finally sponsored a conference on creation and ecology, taking as
their theme 'the eager longing of creation' from Paul's famous
words in his letter to the Romans (Rom 8:19-23), they earned
ridicule for their choice of venue: Limerick in the least accessible
part of the EU for sustainable transport. The committee attracted
further ridicule when they wrote members to get to Limerick via
Michael O'Leary's Ryanair to Shannon Airport. Irish Columban
Seán McDonagh had already remarked in a sermon at St Patrick's
Cathedral, Dublin:

28. For green burials, cf www.arborytrust.org
29. 'Ordination Prayers of Gaul', in *The Ordination Prayers of the Ancient
Western Churches*, H. Boone Porter Jr, ed (London: SPCK, 1967), p 153.
30.Edward P. Echlin, *The Deacon and Creation* (London: The Church Union,
1992) p 19.

Out of one side of the mouth we say that we are stewards of God's creation; out of the other we say, our true home is in heaven. We need to develop a coherent God-talk to underpin our teaching, prayers, worship, and witness. How can this happen when, to the best of my knowledge, not a single theological institution in any of the churches teaches a course in ecological or creation theology.[31]

Nevertheless eco-theology courses – and graduates – now thrive in some universities and theological colleges. Increasingly too, parish priests and ministers lead and encourage inclusive Christian lives and worship.

Matrimony is pre-eminently a community rite. With perennial wisdom, the familiar Genesis stories, introducing our scriptures, portray women and men – with other creatures – together in God's garden earth. We belong together, we complement each other, we leave home and family and garden, and sometimes a community, to be together. We so complement one another that we're like bone from bone, flesh from flesh, the love we share includes the earth entrusted to us – we are *adamah*, of the earth, soil organisms. Humans and humus (and humility) are of the same root. We continue our species. We are responsible, God's image under God, for other creatures of land and sea, which in turn nurture us. The second – and older – Eden story memorably pictures our awesome privileges and responsibilities, women and men together are here to cultivate, observe, serve, and 'guard and keep' God's garden, making sacraments throughout the earth (Gen 2:15). Jesus was familiar with the Genesis teaching and conflated the two accounts when teaching about marriage and divorce (Mk 10:7; Mt 19:5). Paul later described marriage as symbolising the union of Jesus and the church which, as we noticed, is Jesus as community today (Eph 5:31). Every loving, faithful marriage contributes to community, which is why, down the ages, wedding commitments have been religious, or at least community rites and celebration. Every earth inclusive marriage, and every faithful

31. Seán McDonagh, 'Rethinking our Religion, Politics, and Economics', *Doctrine & Life* (November 2008), p 27.

partnership, is a prophetic alternative to individualism oblivious
of community. Single people, same sex partnerships, and religious communities of men or women always include wider relationships of friendship, service, and cooperation of women and
men.

Men and women together, with or without biological children,
are here to facilitate earth's praise of our shared creator (Psalms
147-148). We need not avoid what Sir Jonathon Porritt calls 'the P
word', ever increasing population on a diminishing planet. There
is no more warrant in the Judaeo-Christian scriptures, or in the
living tradition, to procreate beyond a bioregion's carrying capacity than there is to damage climate. Nor is it acceptable to engineer
embryos to increase fertility. When the population 'explosion' became apparent in the 1980s, some Christian environmentalists
proposed 'cosmic marriage', wherein a woman and man share
love caring for the earth, including all children, without necessarily
having several of their own. Cosmic marriage, a prophetic alternative witness, can include fostered children, a woodland, garden, habitat, beach or rescued animals.[32] Parents and single people, teachers, carers, and extended families are challenged as
rarely before to sensitise children to the earth and its needs. In the
wonderland of childhood, children deserve to inhabit wonder, to
cherish their bioregion, gardens, pets, and wildlife, and the great
globe itself. They should learn 'to guard and keep' every special
soil spot entrusted to them and their parents. A venerable illustra-
tion – a picture worth a thousand words – of the earth and climate
love and care we owe our children, is the Jewish Honi story:

> One day Honi was walking down the road. He saw a man
> planting a carob tree. Honi said to him 'Since the carob doesn't
> fruit for seventy years, are you so sure that you'll live seventy
> years and eat fruit from it?' The man replied, 'I found a world
> that was full of carob trees. Just as my ancestors planted for me,
> so I plant for my descendants.' (Babylonian Talmud Ta'anit 23)

The Honi story moves children – and their elders – to realise

---

32. Edward P. Echlin, *The Christian Green Heritage* (Nottingham: Grove
Books, 1989), pp 26-27.

our debt to our Creator, our ancestors, our earth, and trees. Were it composed today, the Talmud doubtless would include the carbon sequestration of food trees, and their reduction of food miles. In our own time and bioregion, Barbara Wood, charismatic daughter of F. W. Schumacher, relates a similar story of a similar man, this time a contemporary French shepherd, who like the Carob man, inspires children – and all of us:

> I am particularly moved by the example an old French shepherd gave. During the first world war, too old to fight for his country, this man spent his time looking after his sheep. But he was filled with the longing to do something for his country in its hour of need. Every day as he minded his sheep he collected acorns and planted them in the scrubland where he grazed his flock. Throughout the war years he planted thousands of trees and today there are acres of forest which give testimony to his act of faith. He, of course, never saw the fruits of his labours. He just did what he believed to be right while he could.[33]

An old man who did what he could, children, and trees is a fitting way to conclude this chapter. Together they keep hope alive, 'there lives the dearest freshness, deep down things'.

33. Barbara Wood, *Our World, God's World* (London: the Bible Reading Fellowship, 1986), p 61.

Conclusion

Will Christ go too, with the world we knew?
And will he come back, when the grass turns black?

Godfrey Meynell

We have the duty to hope.   *Barbara Ward*

During the many meetings preparatory to the 2009 Copenhagen summit, the UNA(UK) convoked a spring conference at the International Maritime Institute overlooking the threatened Thames barrier. Appropriately, as some delegates wryly noted, a sculptured boat greeted us as we entered the building. Also significantly, Lord David Hannay, Chair of UNA(UK), in his address said that Copenhagen was not just a meeting in December. It was already underway and would continue long after the Copenhagen summit of world leaders was over. Hannay's words were correct and compelling even then. Within weeks after the disappointing meeting of world leaders, 'After Copenhagen' and 'Onward to Mexico' meetings of determined people were underway.

If humanity is to avoid global ecocide, and make the transition to sustainable ways of living alternative to fossil fuel driven 'growth' economics, the contribution of all world faiths will be important. During the UNA conference a speaker asked how many delegates were 'faith people'. An impressive number raised hands. Olav Kjorven, Secretary General of UNED, said, 'We indeed see a global mobilisation on climate change across all the major faiths of the world. This is historic and unprecedented.'[1] As creation and incarnation people Christians share concern for God's creation and climate with other faiths. During the still remembered Newbury bypass protests, aptly described by protestors as 'the third battle of Newbury', I spent a weekend visiting camps

---

1. Bill Bowden, 'Climate: The Faiths are Mobilizing', *Church Times* (24 July 2009), p. 9.

and encouraging protestors, some of whom were encamped in trees. On Sunday there was a moving interfaith service at a beautiful doomed tree called 'middle oak'. Christians, Moslems, Jews, Buddhists, Jains and others participated. Someone said 'The wind speaks only through the leaves.' Another added, 'Those in the trees put themselves out on limbs,' to which yet another replied, 'But that's where the action is.' The protestors lost the third battle of Newbury to the 'Roads to Prosperity' juggernaut. But the young protestors and that interfaith service made a durable impact even as, ironically, the destructive bypass does, as it generates more traffic and pollution – and climate change!

Faiths and Water

Interfaith prayer and co-operation will continue. All Faiths, for example, appreciate water as an integral part of creation necessary for life on earth. The Abrahamic faiths testify that when people live sustainably, under God, the heavens bring sweet rain. 'If you walk in my statutes and observe my commandments and do them, then I will give you your rains in their season, and the land shall yield its increase, and the trees of the field shall yield their fruit. And your threshing shall last to the time of vintage, and the vintage shall last to the time for sowing' (Lev 26:3-4). The urban prophet Jeremiah repeats faith in God as the ultimate provider of rain. 'Are there any among the false gods of the nations that can bring rain? Art thou not he, O Lord our God? We set our hope on thee, for thou doest all these things' (Jer 14:22).

Theologian Mary Grey observes that, according to a 2020 report of the UN, 50% of the world will be water stressed by 2032, and Asia, where Grey has worked with women already short of water, will be 90% short of clean water.[2] In 2009, the Alliance of Religions and Conservation (ARC) sponsored a conference at Sarum College, on faith schools and water. Included were conservationists, educators, hydrologists, and water and sanitation agencies. Water crises, of both flood and drought, are increasing even in developed countries. Christians can contribute our tradi-

---

2. Mary Grey, *Sacred Longings, Ecofeminist Theology and Globalization* (London: SCM, 2003), p 26.

tion of the cosmic Jordan. All waters, as the Sarum conference noticed, especially through evaporation and precipitation, are interrelated. All the world's waters, in this sense even literally, are the cosmic Jordan, touched by the Jews, the Baptist, and by God's Word in Jesus. Reverence for the cosmic Jordan, all waters, is expressed especially memorably and appreciatively by the African church father Tertullian. 'It makes no difference whether a person be baptised in a sea or pool, a stream or a font, a lake or a trough; nor is there any distinction between those who John baptised in the Jordan, and those whom Peter baptised in the Tiber.'[3] In a not wholly unrelated incident, people were – and are – amused by the story of a middle aged Irish-born priest (a 'FBI', or 'foreign born Irishman', in American clergy parlance!) who showed little interest in environmental protection, yet always returned sacramental water to a plant near the sacristy. When asked why, he replied 'Because my mother told me to.' I doubt if many good Irish women read Tertullian. But that Irish mother certainly had it right. Respect for water, and its relevance to Christ's own baptism, his life, and death on the cross, where blood and water flowed from his opened side onto the earth, is a major contribution Christians make to water and climate care. In evocative words of the first letter of 'John the elder', 'This is he who came by water and blood, Jesus Christ, not with the water only but with the water and the blood. And the Spirit is the witness, because the Spirit is the truth. There are three witnesses, the Spirit, the water, and the blood; and these three agree' (1 Jn 5:6-7).

Food Security
Closely related to the new appreciation of water, and what we may describe as water security, is the sudden awareness of the fragility of food security. Suddenly, through images on television, despite the way sceptics exploit occasional errors of scientists, we are aware of the melting of the Himalayan glaciers upon which millions depend for irrigation water and food. We are learning about the diminishment of mists and rains from the aptly named

---

3. Tertullian, 'On Baptism', *The Ante-Nicene Fathers, Vol III, Tertullian*, Alexander Roberts, ed (Edinburgh: T.&T. Clark, 1993), pp 670-671.

rainforest, as men continue to fell the trees. There is the threat, and even reality, of rising seas in Australia and East Anglia. And we are beginning to discuss swelling human numbers and migrations that challenge earth's finite resources. These belated discoveries, with warnings of an approaching food crisis by NGOs, scientists, and governments, including in Britain the chief government scientist, have provoked what we may describe as food awareness. Unfortunately, there also remains much indifference, including that of developers, road builders, and 'ground construction' entrepreneurs and those who award planning permissions to destroy fertile soil, including urban soil. Fred Pearce describes damage to precious urban soil, including that of front gardens:

> Soils are being sealed off by being paved over for urban and industrial development, or infrastructure like roads. And when the soil is eventually unsealed many 'brownfield sites' emerge heavily contaminated. This can occasionally be a boon for unusual plants and bugs but more often is a second blight. Urban soils are a resource we may increasingly need ... After years of being taken for granted, food security is suddenly a major political issue.[4]

A few years ago a British Prime Minister announced confidently that Britain could now do away with farming completely. Imports, he said, could supply our food needs. Now such food illiteracy is 'changed, changed utterly. A terrible beauty is born'. Everywhere in the world, in industrialised as well as rural regions, people are learning food's fragility and the need to stabilise climate below an ominous 2° rise for water and food security. Rather less noticed but also urgent is the need to decrease and even eliminate food – and food packaging – waste. Tristram Stuart, who is an authority on food waste, both as pig farmer and a forager in waste bins, warns:

> At last, in recent years governments and corporations have begun to give the problem more attention. A handful of coun-

---

4. Fred Pearce, 'This is Planet Earth', *Your Environment* (Feb-April 2009), p 23.

tries have funded research and campaigns to address food waste, and most of the major supermarkets in Britain have begun to donate a very small proportion of their surplus to charity. But, even now, food corporations keep their waste statistics locked away from the public eye. Waste is their dirty secret. As for solving the problem thoroughly, we have barely begun.[5]

Fortunately, the recent revival of urban food growing not only contributes to food security, it also reduces waste. In summer 2009, for example, I received a call from the Shaftesbury Society charity, now called 'Livability', about a fund raising afternoon to be opened by Sir Christopher Soames, with activities ranging from traditional cream teas and bingo to food stalls and gardening lectures. The organiser said, 'Suddenly, everyone's interested in food, especially local and organic food, including food and faith.' I agreed to give three brief talks on organic fruit and vegetable growing, one explicitly related to Christianity because of Livability's Christian roots. I was privileged to meet many bright people of all ages, interested in helping the less fortunate. Most were interested in organic growing, and especially food security and Christian ecology. Another example of resurgent interest in food growing was the experience of an aspirant allotment grower here in the crowded southeast, who was told by a civil servant with a sense of ironic humour that he would be better advised to apply for a green burial plot, for he would occupy one sooner than he would an allotment. When new allotments are advertised whether by local authorities, the National Trust, or another charity, they are often reserved from the moment they are advertised. We are learning anew the sagacity of James Boswell's aphorism, 'Man is a cooking animal'.[6] And before he cooks he cultivates.

That climate conferences are held in locations such as Stockholm, Rio, Kyoto, Copenhagen, Johannesburg, Bali, Bonn,

5. Tristram Stuart, *Waste, Uncovering the Global Food Scandal* (London: Penguin, 2009), pp 10-11.
6. James Boswell, 'Journal of a Tour of the Hebrides', in Michael Symons, *A History of Cooks and Cooking* (Champagne: University of Illinois Press, 2009), p 34.

London, L'Aguila, Pittsburg, Bangkok, Barcelona, and Mexico City, to mention but a few, shows that the 'cooking animal' is also an urban denizen. And cities historically were founded on fertile, well watered soil. Herbert Girardet observes:

> Urban agriculture can be traced to the world's earliest civilisations. The Sumerians, Aztecs, Mayans and Incas all produced food within their cities, which were usually located on good-quality land with access to water ... London, like Paris, had its own local supplies of fruit and vegetables. Heathrow in west London was a major centre of market gardening until right after the Second World War. Its light, sandy soil is very suitable for vegetable growing ... Florence is still surrounded by orange and olive groves, vineyards and wheat fields, which meet a large proportion of its food requirements. Many cities in Italy, France and Germany still have a very strong relationship to their immediate hinterland, with 'peri-urban' agriculture very much in evidence. Local food production for urban markets continues to be practised in many places. In recent years researchers, politicians and urban planners, particularly in developing countries, have increasingly acknowledged its significance.[7]

Whether in sprawling settlements in crowded southern England, or low density housing in American exurbia, the relationship between cities and their hinterland soil is critical for quality of life and food security. Wendell Berry's words are true not only of middle America, but of cities, towns and villages everywhere: 'The only sustainable city ... would live off the net ecological income of its supporting region, paying as it goes all its ecological and human debts.'[8]

City people grow food in a variety of ways, ranging from containers to gardens, shared open spaces and fields, and allotments. In Vancouver, for example, over 50% of citizens grow some food. Elsewhere some local authorities plant fruit and nut trees along

---

7. Girardet, *Cities, People, Planet*, pp 237-238.
8. Wendell Berry, *Sex, Economy, Freedom and Community* (New York: Pantheon, 1993), p 21.

roads; increasingly in front gardens fruit grows and sprouts sprout again, reminding senior citizens of war and rationing years. My own native Detroit, known as 'the motor city', exemplifies the fertile soil on which most of our cities arose. In once vibrant 'downtown', now largely derelict, the Monroe IHM 'Green Sisters' have inspired and co-ordinated a 'Hope Takes Root' gardening movement whereby inner city people grow food on vacant lots and gardens of abandoned houses. The Sisters' community gardens welcome not only contiguous neighbours but the elderly, infirm, homeless and 'sleeping rough' neighbours. Some, especially the frail, are taught 'square foot gardening' in 'the little land' around them. Sister Elizabeth Walters notes that dozens of families participate, bringing hope to neighbourhood communities. A parallel 'Detroit Agricultural Network' includes family home gardens, community gardens, and twenty school gardens. Some inner city schools teach agri-science, small animal husbandry, and fruit and vegetable growing. Ellen Davis comments, 'If Detroit has become a focus of hope for many of its residents and others around the globe, that is because it demonstrates some of the features that will surely be essential for urban survival.'[9] There are other initiatives in world cities, including notably San Francisco, Havana and Shanghai, which not only contribute to food security, but help to mitigate and adapt to climate damage. Everywhere people must adapt food cultivation to the damage already done by the – sadly still continuing – destruction of much of the earth's most fertile soil, and by intensive agriculture and globalised food trade. In the cities just mentioned, this has begun. Carolyn Steel, specialist in urban culture, says of Britain's perilous food insecurity,

> Contrary to appearances, we live as much on a knife-edge now as did the inhabitants of ancient Rome or *Ancien Régime* Paris. Cities in the past did their best to keep stocks of grain in reserve in case of sudden attack; yet the efficiencies of modern food distribution mean that we keep very little in reserve. Much of the food you and I will be eating next week hasn't even arrived

---

9. Ellen Davis, *Scripture, Culture, and Agriculture*, p 177-178.

in the country yet. Our food is delivered 'just in time' from all over the world: hardly the sort of system designed to withstand a sudden crisis ... Perhaps surprisingly for an island nation, we have never been overly worried about food security in Britain – apart from when German U-boats showed us how vulnerable we were. After the Second World War, the government vowed never to be reliant on food imports again, but 'never' can be a short time in politics. Britain produced just 62 per cent of its own food in 2005, with the figure falling steadily.[10]

We also recognise that there are limits. No human community can be completely 'food secure', for there always threaten tragedies such as climate disruption, disease, war, and with these tragedies, hunger, disease, and death. We must, even in our cities, recover an agrarian lifestyle wherein we live in community, sharing the earth's gifts of food and water, with care for the earth and its creatures. Even in our cities we must care for the soil within, and for the hinterland fields beyond our buildings, always aware of what we may call reliability's limits, an awareness that is lacking in arrogant 'economic growth' cultures. If we care for our soil with respect for its limits we may celebrate with the psalmist in our sustainable cities: 'They establish a city to live in; they sow fields, and plant vineyards, and get a fruitful yield. By his blessing they multiply greatly; and he does not let their cattle decrease' (Ps 107:36-38; Lev 25:36).

An Economy of Life

As we modify lifestyles, with deference to reliability's limits, we will, like a 'transition town' community, be a minority movement. We may take Luke's famous description of the first Jerusalem Christians as our model and inspiration, choosing life together and not the chimera of 'sustainable economic growth': 'All who believed were together and had all things in common; and they sold their possessions and goods and distributed them to all, as any had need. And day by day, attending the temple together and

10. Carolyn Steel, *Hungry City: How Food Shapes our Lives* (London: Vintage Books, 2009), p 100.

breaking bread in their homes, they partook of food with glad and generous hearts, praising God and having favour with all the people' (Acts 2:44-47). We need not literally 'sell and distribute' all our possessions, but we can serve God and our neighbour by a culture of sharing and by following the proximity and in depth principles.

The dominant culture around us of acquisition, growth, and consumption, of 'being competitive' regardless of earth's limits, and of carefree emissions, challenges contemporary prophetic thinkers. At the time of the Copenhagen summit flurry and furore, Mikhail Gorbachev suggested that the developed west needs a *perestroika*, with a dismantling of neo-liberal growth economics. Bishop James Jones of Liverpool said we need 'a dose of economic atheism! We need releasing from the cult of believers dogmatically enslaved to growth.' Archbishop Rowan Williams said we should abandon an economy of growth for one of life, that we should 'choose life'. Timothy Gorringe argues:

> A globally competitive economy means that every firm and every country has to grow in relation to its competitor or it will lose out. When firms announce their annual or even half-yearly profits a return of billions will not satisfy shareholders if it is a few billions less than last year. This need to grow locks the whole world into a suicidal spiral. The claim of the World Trade Organisation (WTO) that economic growth is good for the environment because it shares around cleaner technologies is ludicrous, as the staggering rise in food miles ought to tell us.[11]

An Alternative Economy

Like the first Jerusalem Christians, and like Tim Gorringe, Mikhail Gorbachev, James Jones, and Rowan Williams we can offer a prophetic alternative to the dominant culture of relentless growth. Our society has a way to travel to become a genuine *oikos*, or home, whose law (*nomos*) is love, life, quality, community, and sharing. An alternative economy will be a home community economy which will include other soil creatures, including even those

---

11. Gorringe, *Harvest*, p 18; cf Campaign Against Climate Change, *One Million Climate Jobs Now!*, 5 Caledonian Road, London N1 9DX, 2009, p 25.

invisible mites in a handful of garden soil that work so hard serving our plants and us. We need therefore to restore and protect their habitats, including urban ones. Recent warnings about endangered species – other than our own! – observe that decrease of biodiverse habitats, along with climate change, overdevelopment, and deforestation is a principal danger to the many soil creatures for which, under God, we are responsible. Each of us, and every church or chapel community, can regenerate, nurture, and preserve habitats, whether that be a wildlife friendly garden, a living churchyard, a bird feeder in a care home garden, a hedgerow, woodland, beach, or seabed.

The alternative economy will include people in cities, exurbia, towns and villages. Wherever we live, as we have noticed, our economy, our quality way of living and thriving in community, must be agrarian, caring in community for local soil with all us creatures. That's the way the Bible describes good communities: they include God, whose earth this is, people, the land, and especially the extended family community. And that's the holistic, life choosing way we must live, including the majority who live in densely centralised urban communities. That means each of us who are able will grow some food, which in high density cultures can mean just a few plants or 'square foot garden', while depending for most seasonal food on local hinterland. An urban fruit tree or bush, sprout or kale in season, for example, for a few days reduces inward transport, in addition to being fresher than even local hinterland produce. The ideal of course is many town gardens with plenty of fruit and vegetables – but every productive plant helps.

In a sustainable economy, fruit and nut trees are an important part of the community. Cars will be fewer, electric, and banished from green verges, which will be planted with productive trees. Children will no longer be 'battery reared' and promised a car at 17. Even when some food, such as citrus and bananas are imported we care for their native soil too, buying fairly traded and organic, supporting the fields and small growers from which they come. In brief, we strive to remain palpably within the soil community even when living in centralised settlements.

When people struggle for sustainable economies alternative to dominant consumerism, the word, or at least the concept, that recurs is 'quality'. The alternative economy is one of quality of life, not quantity of things, consumption, acquisition, shopping, bonuses, distant travel. A quality economy eliminates poverty, sharing earth's gifts including personal gifts and talents. The quality economy is the proximity and in depth principles at home. Alternative energies, as in Freiburg, will be common. Homes will be micro-generators, or parts of one. An alternative economy utilises technologies that promote life and commend solidarity and quality. Ruth Conway describes alternative technologies:

> Technologies that contribute to justice are those that are designed to foster respect, understanding, and trust; that encourage solidarity and caring; that guard and celebrate diversity; that enable responsible stewardship rather than exploitation; that meet needs rather than creating wants; that are designed with the paramount question in mind: How will this technology help to serve the righting of relationships within the human community and with nature? These are the technologies that nudge us nearer the sharing and unaffected joy that characterised the earliest Christian community (Acts 2).[12]

In alternative economies of quality, people enjoy not only sustainable technologies but good books, the arts, museums, and continuing education. Where I live, for example, we have annually an 'Academic Inn', similar to an ancient symposium and the meals of Jesus, with drinks, meals, a speaker, and discussion. The most recent – and tenth – was on 'Alternative Living to Growth Economics'. Quality economies also include prayer, a well educated clergy, both married and celibate, good schools and children's worship, appreciation of and care for the elderly and infirm and, not least, the practical arts of cooking and food preserving.

Quality economies include the small and family farms and fisherfolk in our hinterlands. Bob Watson of IAASTD

---

12. Ruth Conway, *Choices at the Heart of Technology, A Christian Perspective* (Harrisburg: Trinity Press, 1999), pp 85-86; cf Tim Jackson, *Prosperity without Growth, Economics for a Finite Planet* (London: Earthscan, 2009) pp 187-204.

(International Assessment of Agricultural Knowledge, Science and Technology for Development) says, 'Business as usual is not an option ... continuing to focus on production alone will undermine our agricultural capital and leave us with an increasingly degraded and divided planet.' Holistic food production includes the welfare of wildlife and all soil creatures, sea life and fisherfolk and water, and the irreplaceable role of women in all areas of food production and preparation and preserving. Patrick Mulvany observes: 'Biologically diverse, agro-ecological farming and grazing methods, especially those practised sustainably by smallscale food producers, particularly women, makes agriculture more resilient, adaptive and capable of eliminating hunger and rural poverty in the long term.'[13]

As Mother Teresa said, we may be a drop in the ocean, but the ocean would be diminished without that drop. Our 'daily bread' or meals are within that drop or contribution we can make. Our meals, including our frequent communal shared meals will consist of local organic food, and follow the LOAF principles (Locally produced, Organically grown, Animal friendly, Fairly traded). Some prefer a vegetarian or vegan lifestyle. Others choose locally reared, perennial grass fed meat, free range fowl, and sustainably caught sea food. Healthy seas, orchards, habitats of various kinds including hedges, woodlands, heath and bogs, sustainable agriculture with perennial pastures sequester rather than increase CO_2. Tristram Stuart notes the unsustainable connections between food wastage, intensive agriculture, and deforestation:

> Forests have to be protected either by internationally enforced conservation measures or by making it more profitable for people to keep their forests intact. In the meantime, it is essential to reduce the demand for resource-intensive foods such as meat, and one of the ways of achieving this is to stop wasting so much. It takes 8.3 million hectares of agricultural land to produce just the meat and dairy products wasted in UK households and by consumers, retailers and food services in the US.

13. Patrick Mulvany, 'Agriculture at a Crossroads: A Summary of the IAASTD Findings', *Agriculture for Development* (Autumn 2008), p 1.

That is seven times the amount of land deforested in Brazil in the past year. Demand for food contributes to the financial incentive to extend agriculture into forests. If we stopped wasting so much it is more likely that this incentive would shrink.[14]

Stuart recognises the perennial need for some landfill, a traditional use of hinterland through human history. Now, however, we need what we may call a waste asceticism. That is, we must reduce drastically the unnecessary waste we discard into landfill or incineration. Disposable nappies, for example, and most packaging are unnecessary. People who send very few containers a year to landfill report their waste is mostly packaging, which cannot be re-used or recycled or composted. Tragically, much plastic waste eventually poisons our fellow creatures, most notoriously in the Pacific gyre. Julian Caldecott reports:

> The central gyre is now a rubbish field as big as Texas, of floating bags, bins, bottles and buckets, flip-flops, dolls, yoghurt pots and polystyrene, fishing nets, nylon lines and floats, wastes that have caused mariners to rename the central gyre as the 'great Pacific garbage patch'. Rather than biodegrading through the action of living things, many of these plastics are only slowly broken down by sunlight, and as they do they become ever-smaller fragments of the same material. At all sizes they are indigestible and useless or worse to life, but smaller fragments are eaten nevertheless, often by jellyfish whose transparent tissues become spangled with internal debris. These then enter the oceanic food chain, ending up in the stomachs of fish, turtles, sea birds and dolphins.[15]

An economy of quality is enriched by the small alternative communities which relate Christ and the church to the land, such as the 'Green Sisters' in North America and Ireland. Here in England we are enriched by the Benedictine Sisters of Stanbrook Abbey, who moved from Worcestershire where the order had lived since 1835 to Crief Farm in the North York moors, rich with monastic tradition. 'There was the footprint of faith all around us

14. Stuart, *Waste*, p 96.
15. Julian Caldecott, *Water: Life in Every Drop* (London: Virgin, 2007), p 66.

and we were renewing it', explains Sister Andrea Savage, 'We were so frantic before we left. But getting here, everything feels right and even the sisters who were worried are happy. It was a dream that has finally become a reality.' The new low carbon abbey maximises solar warmth and light, with its south and west facing windows, and includes a sedum roof with photovoltaic panels for electricity, and includes a wood chip boiler and a large tank for harvested rain water for bathrooms and laundry, and a reed bed for sewage. A vegetable garden and orchard are started. I noticed that trees already have been planted around the abbey and its cemetery. Crief Farm Stanbrook is what every Christian community, including parishes and families can be, a living symbol of sustainability and care for creation. Another shining example is Hilfield Friary in rural Dorset near Dorchester. At Hilfield, Anglican Franciscans are a welcoming centre of a 'project' of friars, priests, and lay people who live and pray in community in partial self sufficiency. Hilfield, like Stanbrook Abbey, is a sustainable witness of a quality local economy. We are further enriched by interfaith communities such as the Lifestyle Community whose motto is 'live simply that others may simply live'. Lifestyle is mostly self sufficient but reminds us that even sustainable communities, including transition towns, need currency for necessary transactions and sustainable, earth caring investment, such as Ecology Building Society, Triodos Bank, and the Co-operative Bank, and Credit Unions.[16]

Three Concluding Principles

All creatures, and all communities, are included and reconciled in the incarnation, 'mysteriously and in very truth, at the touch of the supersubstantial Word the immense host which is the universe is made flesh. Through your own incarnation, my God, all matter is henceforth incarnate.'[17] We and our fellow creatures are included in the mystery that is God in Jesus Christ. Jesus risen remains among us. Three principles can guide us, as we await his return in

---

16. Nona Wright, 'Alternative to Money and the Banking System', *Living Green* (July 2009), pp 31-32.

17. Chardin, 'Mass on the World', in *Hymn of the Universe*, p 24.

the kingdom which includes all creation. First, fertile soil and water are a gift and trust from God, which ultimately belong to God; Second, living and working in community, in service of God, especially in caring for the soil and water, and in production and consumption of food in its various forms, is fundamental to life on earth; Third, misuse of soil or water, and disrupting climate on which all earth creatures depend, are offences against Christ and would unravel any and every political structure or economy. These three principles can guide us to a way of living, an economy of quality, life, love, sharing in community, with gratitude to God our Creator, Sustainer, and reconciler in Jesus. All three principles are exemplified in the prophetic alternative life of Jesus (Mt 5:1-12; Lk 6:20, 23). We also have Paul's famous description of love in his letter to the Corinthians (1 Cor 13:4-7). Harmony with the earth, in community, in an economy of quality, with commitment to Jesus whom we await in hope, is the only genuine progress. We conclude with thoughtful words of David Brower, a founder of Friends of the Earth:

> We may see that progress is not the
> Accelerating speed with which we multiply
> And subdue the earth, nor the growing numbers
> Of things we possess and cling to.
> It is a way along which to search for truth,
> To find serenity and love and reverence for life,
> To be part of an enduring harmony ...

Bibliography

Bailey, Kenneth, *Jesus Through Middle Eastern Eyes* (London: SPCK, 2008).

Barton, Stephen, and Wilkinson, David eds, *Reading Genesis After Darwin* (Oxford and New York: OUP, 2009).

Bauckham, Richard, *Jesus and the Eyewitnesses, The Gospels as Eyewitness Testimony* (Grand Rapids: Wm B. Eerdmans, 2006).

Beerling, David, *The Emerald Planet: How Plants Changed Earth's History* (Oxford: OUP, 2008).

Berry, R. J., ed, *Real Scientists, Real Faith, Seventeen Leading Scientists Reveal the Harmony Between their Science and their Faith* (Simpsonville: Monarch Books, 2009).

Bookless, Dave, *Planetwise: Dare to Care for God's World* (Nottingham: Inter-Varsity Press, 2009).

Brooke, John Hadley, 'The Distinctive Agnosticism of Charles Darwin', *Second Spring*, Vol 8, (2009), pp 49-55.

Caldecott, Julian, *Water, Life in Every Drop, The Causes, Costs and Future of a Global Crisis* (London: Virgin Books, 2007).

Clover, Charles, *The End of the Line, How overfishing is changing the world and what we eat* (London: Ebury Press, 2005).

Conway, Ruth, *Choices at the Heart of Technology, A Christian Perspective* (Harrisburg: Trinity Press, 1999).

Cox, Peter, Rughani, Deepak, Wadhams, Peter, Wasdell, David eds, *Planet Earth We Have a Problem, Feedback Dynamics and the Acceleration of Climate Change* (Leeds: Angus Print, 2007).

Davis, Ellen, *Scripture, Culture and Agriculture: An Agrarian Reading of the Bible* (Cambridge: Cambridge University Press, 2009).

Deane-Drummond, Celia, & Clough, David, eds, *Creaturely Theology, On God, Humans and Other Animals* (London: SCM, 2009).

De Lubac, Henri, *Teilhard de Chardin, the Man and his Meaning* (New York: Burns & Oates, 1967).

Echlin, Edward P., *The Cosmic Circle: Jesus and Ecology* (Dublin: Columba Press, 2004); *Earth Spirituality, Jesus at the Centre* (New Alresford:

Arthur James, 2002); *The Deacon and Creation* (London, The Church Union, 1992); *Changing Climate, Changing Church* (Chapel-en-le-Frith: Catholics for a Changing Church, 2007).

Edwards, Denis, *Ecology at the Heart of Faith* (Maryknoll, New York: Orbis, 2008).

Flannery, Tim, *The Weather Makers, The History and Future Impact of Climate Change* (London: Penguin, 2006).

Freyne, Seán, *Jesus, A Jewish Galilean* (London: Continuum, 2004).

Girardet, Herbert, *Cities, People, Planet, Liveable Cities for a Sustainable World* (Chicheste:, Wiley-Academy, 2004); Girardet, Herbert and Mendonça, Miguel, *A Renewable World, Energy, Ecology, Equality, A Report for the World Future Council* (Dartington: Green Books, 2009).

Grey, Mary, *Sacred Longing, Ecofeminist Theology and Globalization* (London: SCM, 2003); *The Advent of Peace, A Gospel Journey to Christmas* (London: SPCK, 2010).

Guillebaud, John, 'Two sides of the same coin', *Green Christian*, 65 (Summer 2008), pp 8-10.

Gore, Al, *An Inconvenient Truth* (London: Bloomsbury, 2006).

Gorringe, Timothy, *Harvest, Food, Farming, and the Churches* (London: SPCK, 2006).

Gorbachev, Mikhail, *Manifesto for the Earth* (Forest Row: Clairview, 2006).

Harvey, Graham, *We Want Real Food* (London: Constable, 2006); *The Carbon Fields, How Our Countryside Can Save Britain* (Bridgewater: Grass Roots, 2008).

Haught, John, *Deeper Than Darwin* (Boulder: Westview, 2009).

Hodgson, Tony, *Good Food Stories, Our Choices Make the World of Difference* (London: Shepheard-Walwyn, 2006; Farm Crisis Network, 6 Clifford Road, Bexhill TN40 1QA).

Jackson, Tim, *Prosperity without Growth, Economics for a Finite Planet* (London: Earthscan, 2009).

Jamieson, Christopher, 'Might of Metaphysics', *The Tablet* (15 November, 2008), pp 9-10.

Jones, Deborah M., *The School of Compassion: A Roman Catholic Theology of Animals* (Leominster: Gracewing, 2009).

Jones, James, *Jesus and the Earth* (London: SPCK, 2003).

King, Ursula, *Spirit of Fire: Life and Vision of Teilhard de Chardin* (New York: Orbis Books, 1998).

Lane, Dermot, *Challenges Facing Religious Education in Contemporary Ireland* (Dublin: Veritas, 2008).

Lawrence, Felicity, *Eat Your Heart Out* (London: Penguin, 2008).

Lawson, Neil, *All Consuming* (London: Penguin, 2009).

Louv, Richard, *Last Child in the Woods, Saving our Children from Nature Deficit Disorder* (Chapel Hill: Algonquin Books, 2005).

Lynas, Mark, *Six Degrees: Our Future on a Hotter Planet* (London: Harper Perennial, 2007).

McGrath, Alister, *Religion and Scientific Faith: The Case of Charles Darwin's 'Origin of Species'*. The Twenty-fourth Eric Symes Abbott Memorial Lecture (London: King's College, The Dean's Office, 2009).

Marshall, George, *Carbon Detox: Your Step-by-Step Guide to Getting Real About Climate Change* (London: Octopus, 2007).

McDonagh, Seán, *The Death of Life: The Horror of Extinction* (Dublin: Columba, 2004).

Meier, John, *A Marginal Jew: Rethinking the Historical Jesus*, 2 vols (New York: Doubleday, 1991 and 1994).

Messer, Neil, *Selfish Genes and Christian Ethics: Theological and Ethical Reflections on Evolutionary Biology* (London: SCM, 2007).

Monbiot, George, *Heat. How We Can Stop the Planet Burning* (London: Penguin, 2007).

Murray, Robert SJ, *The Cosmic Covenant, Biblical Themes of Justice, Peace and the Integrity of Creation* (London: Sheed & Ward, 1992).

Northcott, Michael, *A Moral Climate, The Ethics of Global Warming* (London: DLT, 2007).

Pope, Stephen, *Human Evolution and Christian Ethics* (Cambridge: CUP, 2007).

Rose, Julian, *Changing Course for Life: Local Solutions to Global Problems* (London: New Evergreen Publishing, 2009).

Shults, F., LeRon, *Christology and Science* (Aldershot: Ashgate Publishing, 2008).

Southgate, Christopher, *The Groaning of Creation: God, Evolution and the Problem of Evil* (Louisville: Westminster John Knox, 2008).

Speaght, Robert, *Teilhard de Chardin, A Biography* (London: Wm Clownes & Sons, 1967).

Steel, Carolyn, *Hungry City, How Food Shapes Our Lives* (London: Vintage, 2008).

Stern, Nicholas, *Blueprint for a Safer Planet, How to Manage Climate Change and Create a New Era of Progress and Prosperity* (London: Bodley Head, 2009).

Stuart, Tristram, *Waste, Uncovering the Global Food Scandal* (London: Penguin, 2009).

Teague, Ellen, *Becoming a Green Christian* (Stowmarket: Kevin Mayhew, 2009).

— *Our Earth, Our Home: Green Assemblies for key stages 1-2* (Stowmarket: Kevin Mayhew, 2009).

Toolan, David SJ, *At Home in the Cosmos* (NY: Orbis, 2003).

Viviano, Benedict OP, *The Kingdom of God in History* (Wilmington: Michael Glazier, 1988).

Wood, Barbara, *Our World, God's World, Reflections for Advent and the Christmas Season on the Environment* (London: The Bible Reading Fellowship, 1986.

Wright, Christopher J. H., *God's People in God's Land: Family, Land and Property in the Old Testament* (Grand Rapids: Eerdmann, 1990).